*In Search of the Past*

# THE DESIRE TO PLEASE

KILLYLEAGH CASTLE, COUNTY DOWN

*Frontispiece*

# The Desire to Please

## A STORY OF HAMILTON ROWAN AND THE UNITED IRISHMEN

by

*HAROLD NICOLSON*

"The desire to please,—a desire which tempts us to design
an imaginary portrait of ourselves. Which is weakness."

ALAIN. *Propos sur l'éducation.*

NEW YORK

HARCOURT, BRACE AND COMPANY

# TABLE OF CONTENTS

# LIST OF ILLUSTRATIONS

# PROLOGUE

## (1)

WHEN I unlock the cupboards of my memory, I wonder sometimes why it is that the shelves on which are stored the relics
of my childhood days in Ireland should retain their scent with
special vividness, or should give to my searching fingers a
different tenderness of touch. The other shelves are packed
with memories more interesting, more numerous and more
diverse; yet as, in the half-darkness, my mind gropes out to
grasp the small bundle of my Irish associations, I am conscious of quite separate stirrings of affection and regret.

It is not that I identify with Ireland alone the happiness of
my dawn-golden days. I experienced intenser moments of
felicity in other lands. It is not even that the smooth texture
of my Irish holidays was severed suddenly from the rougher
tweed of adult life or that upon the word "Ireland" there
still glisten for me the unbrushed drops of dew. It is, I
think, that I retain a distaste for the nomad existence imposed
upon my first thirty years and that the homes of my mother's
family in Ireland represent for me that sedentary element,
those centres of continuity, which without knowing it, I missed
through all those years.

The Nicolsons have for many generations been a landless
tribe. I am prepared to believe (in fact I like to believe) that
the founder of the family was a Norwegian of the name of
Nicolas'sen, whose descendants established their ascendancy
over the Hebrides and ruled in Lewis and in Skye. Their
correct Norwegian name was Nicolsen or Nicolson but they
developed a tendency in later years to assume the local, but
less correct, form of MacNicol. Professor Skene, who identi-
fies them with the Karinoi of Ptolemy's *Geographia*, informs

us in his *The Highlanders of Scotland* that the name of "Mac-Nicol is sometimes pronounced Macreacail." I am glad that this pronunciation has since lapsed.

All that we know with any certainty is that Andrew Nicolsen established himself upon the promontory of Totternish in Skye, where he constructed the stronghold of Scorrybreck and gathered around him the majority of his clansmen. They remained there for eight hundred years. They are there to-day. And although the House of Scorrybreck is no more than a heap of stones among the heather, looking down upon the Mull of Raasay, yet the Nicolsons still flourish in the Island and their names figure numerously upon its war memorials or upon the butcher carts and milk vans which ply from Portree. As the centuries progressed the clan dispersed and lost their lands. The Shiant Islands, it is true, floating diaphanous in the Little Minch, are today the property of my younger son; yet he obtained them neither by inheritance nor by conquest, but because the call of the blood, or some innate romanticism, induced him to purchase these lovely lonely islands by a cheque drawn upon Barclay's Bank at Oxford. There they stand none the less, uninhabited but loved; in the night-time their great basalt cliffs hum like organ pipes to the moan of nesting puffins; in the day-time when the sun breaks through the veil of mist, the rain-drops sparkle upon the downs and heather, and when one sings aloud the seals come out upon the rocks below and tumble their happy little faces in the surf.

My own branch of the MacNicols, or Nicolsons as they were more correctly called, left Skye in 1570 and established themselves as lawyers in Edinburgh where they acquired riches and land, served successively as Lord Provost, and bought the two valuable properties of Carnock and Tilli-coultrie. The old house of Carnock, with its plaster ceilings, its sloping corridors, its castellated walls, still stands as I write these words. But the incursions of a coal-mine have sapped its foundations and at any moment it may totter or be pulled to the ground. For long I believed the legend that my forebears were robbed of their properties in Nicolson Square and Nicolson Street in Edinburgh; of the old house of Carnock and the pleasant meadows of Tillicoultrie, owing to the fact that they took the wrong side in 1715 or 1745. I suspect that Miss Plimsoll (who, like all governesses, had a weakness for the Jacobites) imprinted this legend upon my pliant mind. I can find no evidence to support it. What really happened was that Sir Thomas Nicolson the fourth baronet, who was also the fourth Lord Napier and Ettrick, died childless, his estates and his peerage passed to his aunt who was heiress to both of them in the female line; and the baronetcy slid aside to his landless collaterals, my own immediate forebears, who were then serving in the Scottish Regiment in the Low Countries. That was a dull thing to happen. Nor can I summon up any interest in the succeeding generations who lived Dutch lives, were buried at Breda or at Ypres, and thereafter became wholly denationalized, crossing to England, and serving as soldiers or sailors under Hanoverian Kings.

My grandfather, Admiral Sir Frederick Nicolson, lived in a little house in William Street, off Lowndes Square, in London. It was a displeasing house; it could never have suggested any home. The lace curtains of the drawing room smelt of coal dust, and gave upon a balcony, the railing of which left a layer of soot upon the hand. If one leant forwards, one could see the carriages passing in and out of Albert Gate. In the back room there was a cottage piano on the lid of which was inlaid in rosewood the semblance of a large marine shell. Above it hung a row of yellow photographs of distinguished musicians bought in Dresden before the Franco-Prussian war. My grandfather was a fierce and selfish old man with a raucous voice; he spent most of his retirement reading French novels at the Travellers Club. There was little sense of a family home about William Street; on the few occasions that we stayed there we had the feeling of being provisional, unwanted, grubby, and in the way.

My father during all the years of my childhood and boyhood lived abroad. From Persia, where I was born, he went to Constantinople; from Constantinople to Budapest; from Hungary to Sofia; from Bulgaria to Morocco; from Morocco to Madrid and from Madrid to Russia. Such continuity as my home life possessed was provided for me by the objects which my parents would carry with them on their several migrations. There were the Persian embroideries; the brass camel and the rugs which they had bought in the bazaars at Istanbul; the bowl of a hookah into which I had inserted a piece of india-rubber where it rattles, hardened and inextricable, to this day; the Arundel prints; the two oil paintings representing Hungarian peasants driving with alacrity across the Nagy Alföld; the photographs of immediate relations; and the Turkish table of mother of pearl, sitting cross-legged upon which I had been painted as a child. The pantechnicon vans would roll across the Caspian, the Mediterranean or the Aegean, and there, in a house which looked, now upon the Andrassy Strasse, now upon the Golden Horn, now towards Trafalgar, or now across the Neva to the fortress of St. Peter and St. Paul, the Nicolson home would be reconstructed. Behind this exotic tapestry there was a gap of which only today am I fully conscious. What I really wanted was to see the trees grow year by year in fields that had known me since I could not walk. I wanted to come back after long absence and to mourn the fall of a familiar elm or rejoice to find that the willow cuttings had shuffled into a coppice of their own. I longed instinctively to feel a little less un-English in my own country, a little less foreign when abroad. I hated this sense of unceasing dispersal; I wanted to be localized and concentrated; I wanted to feel autochthonous, the son of some hereditary soil. It was for this reason, I repeat, that the holidays that I spent with my mother's people over in Ireland assumed so deep a meaning for me; and that I came to look upon Clandeboye, Killyleagh and Shanganagh as anchors in a drifting life, as the only places where I ceased to be a pot-plant for ever being bedded out in alien soil.

For years I cherished the illusion that if I belonged anywhere I belonged to Ireland. It was a shock to me to discover that here also my people were but settlers in a foreign land. My mother's family had, it is true, lived in Ireland for three hundred years and many of them (including my own mother) had gone, permanently, unashamedly, passionately, native. Yet slowly and painfully it was borne in upon me that they and their fellow immigrants were also living among foreigners and that here also I must fail to find the special authenticity, the earth-harmony for which I longed.

(2)

At Clandeboye [1] the Protestant ascendancy was established, unmitigated, unperturbed. The gravel upon the garden-paths stretched weedless between mown grass; the men who raked it would touch their hats as the carriages crackled by. The gates which opened on the deer park, or barred the roads which led to Bangor or to Helen's Tower, were firm upon their hinges; they closed with a soft click; the angles of the cross-bars remained sticky for weeks with fresh white paint. The flag flew from Helen's Tower, the bell rang for church, the curate propped his bicycle against one of the stone cannon-balls at the entrance to the house; and at 11.15 each morning the butler would enter the library bringing cake and Marsala, the London newspapers and the English mail.

Beyond the woods and lakes of Clandeboye, outside the walls and fencing which enclosed the demesne, Ireland asserted her eternal shambling sway. As one got farther and farther away from Belfast or Bangor the gates were tied with

[1] See *Helen's Tower*, the first volume of this series.

flax, the white-washed walls would tumble down across the road-way, the gorse-bushes flamed in the fields. There were strange people in those parts, I heard it whispered, out over there by Downpatrick or Ballynahinch, or where the soft tides of Strangford Lough leave behind them flats of sea-weed spreading the scent of iodine and the cry of gulls in the moist air. There were "Catholics" in those parts, not many of them it was true, but dangerous people, difficult people, people who were in the hands of the fenians and the priests; alien, intractable, sly. Even as a child I had felt vaguely that here was the "foreign" element which had disturbed me so much in Turkey, Bulgaria or Morocco. "What *are* the Catholics?" I would ask Miss Plimsoll. "No, dear," she would answer, "no, dear, you must not ask me that." "Is Dick Larson a Catholic?" I would persist. "Really," she would snap, "what extraordinary ideas you get into your head. Most extraordinary." Here again was a forbidden subject. I would trot down to the carpenter's shop and ask my friend Tom Moore. He was a fervent orangeman and the question was not well placed. "They are evil men," he would say, gazing at me above his spectacles with angry blue eyes, "they are evil men." So here also was a mystery and here also something aloof and hostile beyond the warm orbit of my family life.

It was our custom, in the summer holidays, or when my mother was at Clandeboye, to drive the twelve miles to Killyleagh. That was the home in which she had been born and bred and I could tell by the movements of her little hands that she was excited by these expeditions and a trifle flustered. At Clandeboye she was always the youngest sister, even as at Shanganagh she was treated always as the youngest daughter, and in her infinite selflessness, in her gentle grace of self-effacement, she accepted the position with affection. But when we drove to Killyleagh and the tang of the sea-weed first breathed across the fields, shy birds of memory would stir in her heart. It was not that she became self-assertive (she could never have been self-assertive) it was that she became strangely self-possessed. As we passed from the ordered propriety of Clandeboye out into the wild untidiness of the Ards she would glance at my father with affectionate amusement, knowing that here was something that she understood which he, for all his wisdom, could never understand. And then she would cry to us, "Do you feel it? Do you feel it? The scent of the sea-weed in the air?"

Year after year we would go upon these expeditions, sometimes returning that same evening with the sun flaming on the low levels of the Lough, or sometimes remaining a night or two at Killyleagh when from my turret window I could see below me the lantern of the Clandeboye coachman as he tended his horses in a strange stable. I recall particularly the last occasion on which I went to Killyleagh with my father and mother. I was older then and it was my last year at school. I have been there only once in later life, wandering as a man amid deserted gardens and fallen parapets while a December wind howled across from Scotland round the towers. Our last family expedition took place in August. My uncle Dufferin was dead by then and the lavish establishment of Clandeboye had been much reduced. We hired a landau from the livery stable at Bangor. Slowly, in that musty vehicle, we clopped along the roads of County Down. And then once again, as I had always remembered, my mother began to stir excitedly and to make little bird-like movements with her hands. "Do you feel it?" she exclaimed again. "Do you feel it? The scent of sea-weed in the air?"

I sat there as the landau rumbled slowly along, sniffing politely, but uncertain whether I approved of the excitement in my mother's eyes. My sister, who was but seven years old at the time, sat between my father and mother, unconscious of any change of atmosphere. My father was quietly amused. It was then that the incident occurred.

We were approaching Killyleagh and the towers of the castle were already visible above the fold of the hill. Suddenly from the hedge beside the lane darted a scare-crow woman yelling words which seemed imprecations but which were in fact phrases of welcome and love. Her grey hair streamed down her haggard face; the rags that she wore barely covered her skeleton ribs; she clambered upon the carriage step stretching a naked arm towards my mother, slavering toothless cries. My father, although a courageous man, drew back in startled dismay. My sister screamed in panic fear. But my mother was overjoyed. "Oh Meg!" she exclaimed, the tears already running down her cheeks. "Oh Meg dear—how clever of you to know me after all these years!" The harridan still clung to the carriage emitting Irish cries. "It's only Mad Meg," my mother said to us almost crossly. My father fumbled in his pocket and pressed silver into the twitching jerking hand. Meg flung herself from the carriage and fell backwards into the ditch shouting affection at my mother. "My darlint," she screamed, "my little darlint." We drove under the Castle gateway and into the quiet of the fore-court. We all wore different expressions. My father looked embarrassed but amused. My sister was still gasping from the paroxysm of fear which had assailed her. I felt disgusted and disturbed.

My mother behaved most strangely. She was still half-laughing and half-crying and her hat had been twisted to one side by Meg's attempts at an embrace. My father drew her attention to this unseemly fact. She replaced her hat, not as women should, with a gesture of careful adjustment the two elbows being held jointly aloft, but by an almost vicious dab or poke. For what did hats matter now that one was back at Killyleagh, that one was fifteen again, and that Mad Meg had jumped to kiss one after thirty years? We rang the bell in a dazed state of mind; the great door opened; our feet echoed upon the polished floors of Killyleagh. We regained our composure.

But as I climbed the staircase (that very staircase down which, as I shall relate, the drunken Ursula was tumbled out into the night) I was conscious, for by then I was as much as seventeen years of age, that Mad Meg had made a difference. Ireland herself, the Ireland to which all these years I had thought that I belonged, had also become a foreign country inhabited by people who uttered cries. My mother's relations might be almost native after all those centuries. Once again I was different; even from her.

## (3)

My father had a friend who was a member of the Gaelic League. I should say more accurately that we suspected him of being associated with that sinister society, since he would attend rebel meetings, dress himself from time to time in a saffron kilt, try desperately to learn the Irish language, and never cease to abuse Dublin castle and to refer to us (agreeably enough, but to the dismay of my mother) as "you English." He was a tall, rather untidy man, who concealed his nationalist convictions and the fact that he had not made much of his public opportunities, under a bantering manner such as rendered it difficult for the young to decide whether he was being serious or not. He believed, for instance, in the existence of fairies, whom he called "the little people," and was in fact convinced that in the wood behind his house there was a fairy circle round which, on certain nights of the year, the little people danced by star-light. I was warned that I must make no mock of this superstition since if I did so he would rise suddenly and slam the door. But he was a nice man, a jovial man, and he was generous with his gifts.

His name was Lord Castletown and in the 'sixties he had been my father's most intimate friend at Oxford. Their paths had diverged since then but they had maintained their friendship and when they met they would each relapse into the facetiousness of their Brasenose days, becoming suddenly so different that their wives gazed at them with an anxious stare.

The Castletowns lived at Doneraile in County Cork and during his summer leave my father would invariably (having dumped his family at Clandeboye, Killyleagh or Shanganagh) spend three weeks or so visiting the seats of his Irish friends, always devoting one of these three weeks to Doneraile. When my Uncle Dufferin died, and when my grandmother at Shanganagh grew too old for numerous company, this dumping process became more difficult; and so one year, when I was eighteen years of age, we all went down to Doneraile for the month of August. It was there that I understood that there was an Ireland, perhaps even the real Ireland, which was very different either from Co. Wicklow or from Co. Down.

There was a little room or study to the right of the hall at Doneraile which interested me extremely. It was in the closet adjoining this room that in 1717 or so Elizabeth St. Leger, daughter of the then Lord Doneraile and subsequently Mrs. Aldworth, spied through a crevice in the brickwork when her father was holding a masonic meeting. According to an alternate version of the story she had concealed herself in the clock-case. Her presence was discovered and it was decided that the only way to surmount the difficulty was to make Elizabeth a Freemason herself. She thus shares with Mrs. Beaton of Norwich and Madame de Xantrailles (who spied similarly upon the Frères Artistes in Paris), the distinction of being one of the only three women who have ever penetrated the masonic mysteries. There is a portrait of her in her masonic robes, and her apron and regalia are preserved in the family. Lord Castletown was fond of this story and would tell it with glee, partly because it disturbed my father to be told stories about secret societies and partly because it embarrassed Lady Castletown to feel that any member of her family (for she was born a St. Leger) could have behaved with such duplicity.

I was interested in the story and one morning, when my father had gone out, I asked Lord Castletown to show me exactly how Mrs. Aldworth had perpetrated her fell deed. He took me into the room which he used as a study and there upon the table I observed a bundle of cuttings from the nationalist papers. They referred to a particularly lurid scandal at Dublin Castle. I hesitated whether to read them but Lord Castletown encouraged me. "Go on," he said, "read that muck. It will show you how we people here are governed." I was not particularly impressed by the story, since I believed, as I still believe, that it was totally untrue. But I was impressed by the fact that when a step sounded in the passage, which Lord Castletown may have mistaken for my father's, he bundled the cuttings together and hid them rapidly in a drawer. A sense of furtiveness and conspiracy, appropriate to that little room, was given to the scene. I was entranced. I found, as any boy would find, the atmosphere of rebellion plus secret societies, plus masonic lodges more congenial than the garden parties at Shanganagh or the luncheons to which I was sometimes (although very rarely) invited at Private Secretary's Lodge in Phoenix Park. Something, I realized, was going on underneath—something of which my mother's family would not approve. But Lord Castletown for his part was so flustered by the incident that he forgot to tell me how exactly Elizabeth St. Leger arranged her peep-hole. I question moreover whether he really knew.

Those were happy weeks, those weeks at Doneraile. During the day time I could shoot buck, or wander round the surrounding country, or just sit and read. I remember particularly one hot afternoon when it rained in torrents and we all sat after luncheon in the winter garden, inhaling the smell of the tube roses, listening to the rattle of the rain upon the glass roof, listening to the gentler tinkling of the fountain as it splashed among the ferns. My mother knitted. Lady Castletown played patience on a square green table. My father tried in vain to interest Lord Castletown in the necessity of improving Anglo-French relations and Lord Castletown (who

was more than slightly deaf) would reply in terms expressive
of the long iniquities of the English Government and the un-
ending sufferings of the patient Irish people. And I read the
works of Edmund Spenser.

## (4)

I am not one of those who claim that they enjoy the *Faerie
Queene*. I detest allegory in any form; I do not care for deliberate archaism; I hate the catch-word jingles at the top;
I am bored and bewildered by the whole story; nor do I find
that any Spenserian stanzas "elope with ease"—on the contrary I find that they stick like burrs to the tongue. It was
not from any love of his poetry that I read the *Faerie Queene*
upon that wet August afternoon, but because Kilcolman Castle,
where Spenser lived, was only a few miles from Doneraile.
I had been there upon the day before and sat for an hour
among "the green alders by the Mulla's shore," looking up
from the bogs and marshes to the Mole, or down to where
a ruined keep marks all that remains of the house in which,
on a famous occasion, Spenser entertained Sir Walter Raleigh.
I had always supposed that Spenser was a nice little cropped-
haired man and I deemed it hard that he should have "been
called from faerie land to struggle through dark ways." But
as I turned the cloying pages of the *Faerie Queene*, I found
that in my edition was also printed "A view of the present
state of Ireland." I read this aggressive pamphlet with dismay. I went back to the house and brought other books,
notably Mr. Church's well written but apologetic biography
in the English Men of Letters Series. I discovered that
Edmund Spenser had not been mild or loveable at all. Not
only had he been rapacious himself, but he heartily approved
of rapacity in others. His hero was that Lord Grey de Wilton
who at Smerwick had massacred the Italian soldiers after they
had surrendered to his mercy. Spenser had no sympathy at
all for Irish Nationalism. He looked upon the owners of the

country as "vile catiff wretches, ragged, rude, deformed." He blamed the comparative failure of the *Faerie Queene*, not upon his own lack of constructive power, but upon the unfortunate Irish people. He called it:

"The wilde fruit which salvage soil hath bred,
Which being through long warres left almost waste,
With brutish barbarism is overspread."

He definitely advocated massacre as a solution of the Irish problem and he was furious with Queen Elizabeth who had the humanity and sense to see that Lord Grey de Wilton had gone too far, and might bring her good name into disrepute with foreign courts. I felt almost relieved when I read how he had been caught at Kilcolman by Tyrone's rebellion, how the Irish had sacked his house and burnt it to the ground, and how, escaping to England, he had died of shock almost upon the very day that he reached London. "Mild Spenser, indeed," I snorted to my mother, "why the man was worse than Joseph Chamberlain." My mother merely gave a twitch to the skein of wool she was knitting and smiled up at me in affectionate disregard.

Lord Castletown, that evening, agreed with me that it was very wrong, very wrong indeed. But nothing to what was happening at Dublin Castle at that very moment. This over-statement created an awkward pause, and to break it my father advised me to read Lecky. I did read Lecky, volume after volume, since they are handy to hold. And it was then that I learnt that my mother's forebears had behaved in no way better than Edmund Spenser. They had behaved even worse, since they had been more successful. After all, Killyleagh was a great house, still boasting of its battlements and its Jacobean door. Not only had the Hamiltons been as greedy as any of the undertakers, as any of the Ulster planters, but they had profited by their loot. All except one of them. There was one man who stood out from the greedy, grabbing horde. A man called Hamilton Rowan of Killyleagh Castle had sought, at the end of the eighteenth century, to redress this wrong. Lecky spoke of him as "foolish and impulsive, but also brave, honourable, energetic and charitable, a man of great physical strength and beauty, always ready to meet any opponent with his pistol, and to throw himself headlong into adventures."

"Who," I said to my mother eagerly, "tell me, who was Hamilton Rowan?"

"He was my great-grandfather," she said. "He was a rebel. We do not talk about him much." She smiled and twitched at her wool. "I think," she added reminiscently, "that we are rather ashamed of him in a way."

### (5)

I must, I suppose, have heard his name mentioned before. Yet a child's powers of identification, acute though they be within the tiny ambit of immediate perception, are fluctuating indeed when extended in space or time. Nor did I as a child possess that sense of the incongruous which should have suggested to me that it was strange that among the many Rowan Hamiltons who surrounded or preceded my mother there should have been one alone who reversed his surname and called himself Hamilton Rowan. When I came to read his autobiography I remembered well enough my grandmother telling me a story of a man who escaped from prison. A revenue cutter had come alongside the little boat in which he was escaping from Ireland and had dropped into the stern a proclamation offering £2,000 reward for his arrest; the boatmen, according to my grandmother's version, had been too noble to betray him; scorning such blood-money, they had sped for France. I remember dimly being told this story, but the expression "revenue cutter" had, I suppose, twitched my mind away from Ireland and towards a different nucleus of associations, centering around Walmer, and Romney Marsh and the brave old smuggling days. I did not realize that my grand-

mother was telling me a cautionary tale about a member of
my family. It made but slight impress on my mind.

I was aware, however, that floating as an amoeba in the
backwaters of my memory, was another recollection, associated dimly with the ash-pit at Shanganagh and an ancestor of
whom my friend Dick Larkin wanted me to feel ashamed.
I was perplexed by the prominence assumed in this pattern
by the ash-pit at Shanganagh. The unpleasant conversation
with Dick Larkin did not, I am convinced, occur at the ash-
pit, but upon the beach by the Martello Tower almost a mile
away. To reach the avenue which led down to the beach one
had to pass the ash-pit, but the conversation which ensued
was not connected with it and should by rights be associated
in my mind with the crunch of shingle or the crackle of dried
sea-weed stranded by the winter gales. The ash-pit, which
abutted on the door towards the stables and was surrounded
by low but still castellated walls, aroused my childish squeam-
ishness. For when, some thirty years later, I revisited Shanganagh and turned the corner on my slow walk to the remembered sea, I was checked suddenly in the gentle flow of memories by the apprehension of something immediate and dis-
quieting. My childhood's distaste must have been strong indeed to have darted out at me after thirty years and I can
only assume that the fear and displeasure occasioned by Dick
Larkin's revelation on the beach must have reached back to the
earlier repugnance caused by passing the hated ash-pit thirty
minutes before.

I must have been eight years old at the time, since Dick
Larkin, who was six months older than myself, had already
been one term at school. He adopted towards me that informed but charitable manner (a manner which in an even
more horrible shape he adopts towards me today) indicating
that although he was now at school and I still in the nursery
yet he was fond of children in his way. Courteously, neatly,
protectively he accompanied me past the ash-pit and along the
tree-lined lane that led to the beach. He treated my remarks

with kindly but emphatic patience until I longed to rub his nose in mud. I know we had an argument; I suppose I was rude; I suppose I made some wounding reference either to his father, his mother, or his home. Because, when we reached the beach, he gazed thoughtfully at Bray head and murmured, half to himself, "Well in any case, none of *my* people have been hanged."

I gazed at him in stupefaction. "Don't you know," he hissed vindictively, "that your grandfather was hanged?"

I can remember vividly the shock which this revelation, first uttered in an undertone, and then repeated in an angry hiss, created in my mind. I cannot remember what I answered. I do not recall how we walked back, what happened when we repassed the ash-pit, or how long I hid this dreadful secret in my heart. I do recall, however, that in some later moment of confidence I asked my mother why grandpapa had been hung. She went on knitting and gradually elicited the Dick Larkin revelation. "It was only your great-great-grandfather," she said, "and he wasn't really hanged; he escaped just in time."

"But why?" I persisted, only slightly comforted.

"He was convicted," she said, "of High Treason."

That sounded grand. Had I known that I could have floored Dick Larkin on the beach. I was pleased by my mother's explanation and my anxiety regarding my great-great-grandfather dropped back into the calm depths of consciousness. It was not till ten years later, in the winter garden at Doneraile, that the name "Hamilton Rowan" started out at me from the pages of Lecky and stirred the sleeping pool.

### (6)

The indignation to which I was stirred that August afternoon at Doneraile by the wrongs of Ireland and the iniquities of my forebears did not for long retain its flaming form. I returned to England, and from then onwards I became involved in other interests and in other wrongs. Ireland receded from my foreground, becoming the dim island in the west, rarely visited, detached from the hurry of my later life, yet rich with affective associations, in which the fictions of my childhood mingled with the illusions of my adolescent life. It is not that my distaste for rapacity or my hatred of violence have declined; but in my adult years I transferred my sympathies to those small countries which were oppressed by Governments other than my own.

My preoccupation with Hamilton Rowan remained a fairly constant element of interest. I read and reread his published Autobiography, seeking to discover some central meaning in that jumbled memoir, hoping to find some clue to his aberrations—*cherchant pourquoi il voulait tant s'évader de la réalité*. I consulted the works and manuscripts of his contemporaries, only to find that their witness was disconcertingly affable and vague. I have pushed my researches further. In this I have been aided by my cousin, Hans Rowan Hamilton, who has for years been accumulating unpublished material and who with rare generosity has placed the fruit of his labours at my disposal. In the chapters that follow I have striven to give some coherent form to the narrative which I have pieced together. But the enigma remains.

Through disillusion, through betrayal, through danger of death, through poverty, through exile, through humiliation Hamilton Rowan was taught that even the noblest ideas, if ill-controlled, become as hurricanes whirling a man's egoism to his own destruction. He should have learnt that among the flotsam and jetsam of history there are few more pitiful figures than the hero who fails to remain heroic. Yet he lived on to the age of eighty-four unconscious of what had happened, still bowing to the huzzas of the mob, still wearing upon his features a smile of self-satisfaction. The problem of his astounding unawareness remains unanswered.

Although I have often felt irritated by Hamilton Rowan, I have never felt estranged from him. There are facets of his character, incidents in his career, in which, with a start of dismay, I recognized myself. Had fate decreed, as she might so easily have decreed, that I should live in Ireland from 1860 to 1942: had I inherited Shanganagh Castle from my grandmother: had I spent my middle years in that gothic abode, nestling among flowering chestnuts at the foot of the Wicklow mountains; then to me also it might have happened that the spell of Ireland stole my wits away. I also might have found myself at variance with kith and class and creed; I also might have donned the saffron kilt and joined the Gaelic League; I also might have found myself edging closer and closer to Yeats or AE or Lady Gregory and have been lost in the mists of the Abbey Theatre; and I also might have been lured by sympathy into association, by association into conspiracy, and by conspiracy into treason. Finding myself in a false position from the outset, finding that although *with* the Irish, I was not *of* the Irish, I should have been forced by loyalty to their cause to be even more extreme than they were. It might have been that after the Easter rebellion I was shot by English rifles at Kilmainham Jail. It might have been that I escaped to America, returned in 1923, changed my name to Macreacail, and become Under Secretary of Fine Arts in the De Valera Government. But more probably, when England found herself in danger in 1914, there would have come a sharp jerk at my heart. I should have recoiled from the path that I had followed, abjured my heresies, and made my peace (as Hamilton Rowan made his peace) with the mammon of unrighteousness and His Majesty's Government in the United Kingdom.

In that event I should have been allowed by Mr. de Valera to retain my house and woods at Shanganagh, to remain a mumbling member of the Kildare Street Club, and to walk on summer evenings down the lone avenue to the sea-shore, my feet crunching on the dried sea-weed of the beach—mistaken, unsatisfactory, angry and very old.

# I

## PARENTAGE AND EDUCATION,
### 1751–1767

The Hamiltons of Ulster–The Vicar of Dunlop and his sons–The plantation of Co. Down–Conversation Piece–Mrs. Hamilton–Mr. Rowan–Birth and early education of Hamilton Rowan–Mr. Fountain's school and Rathbone Place–Gawen Hamilton of Killyleagh–Westminster School–Contemporary accounts of Hamilton Rowan–Dr. Lucas–Mr. Rowan's will–Influences which moulded Hamilton Rowan's character–His defect of unawareness.

## (1)

THE HAMILTONS are of Scottish origin and attribute their early energy to the founder of their particular branch, the Reverend Hans Hamilton, Vicar of Dunlop, an illegitimate scion of the ducal house. This clergyman is described by his contemporaries as being "a very hopeful youth, of good parts and disposition." He was of such good disposition that he had the foresight to acquire influence with James VI while Queen Elizabeth still reigned. He had six sons, of whom the eldest, James Hamilton, crossed to Dublin, became a Fellow of Trinity College, and opened a Latin school in Great Ship Street. On the accession of King James, Hamilton transferred himself to London where he became one of the many mendicant Scottish courtiers on the prowl for Irish grants. It does not appear that the King showed any immediate solicitude for the eldest son of his old friend the Vicar of Dunlop. In fact, at the lavish distribution of Irish lands which occurred after the "flight of the Earls," it was James Hamilton's cousin, and not James himself, who was accorded large properties

19

in Tyrone and created Earl of Abercorn. James Hamilton
retired from the court in angered jealousy. "He made great
use," records the Hamilton Manuscript, "of a public gout or
gravel, that he might hide himself in his house gown." Eventually a fresh, if tortuous, opportunity was offered to him
owing to the intemperance of Con O'Neill. In a fit of drunkenness this young chieftain, accompanied by his fellow revel-
lers, delivered an attack on Belfast Castle. He was arrested
and confined at Carrickfergus, but was allowed to entertain
his friends and in fact to wander about the little town. Hugh
Montgomery, Lord of Braidstone, hearing of this escapade,
sent an emissary to Con O'Neill at Carrickfergus offering to
intercede for him at Whitehall and even to obtain his pardon. In return O'Neill was to assign to Montgomery all
his properties in Southern Clandeboye. James Hamilton was
outraged by this iniquitous bargain. He journeyed at once
to Whitehall, was able to persuade the then ageing King that
the transaction was in fact disreputable, and to put before him
what seemed an equitable compromise. The Montgomery
grant was transferred to James Hamilton, on condition that
he assigned one third of the properties to Hugh Montgomery
and handed back the remaining third to Con O'Neill. The
latter, being clearly a feckless young man, immediately resold
his third share to James Hamilton who then crossed to Ulster
to take possession. He established himself at Bangor, built a
large house at Holywood and bought from the Whytes the
lands of Dufferin on the western shores of Strangford Lough.
At Killyleagh, perched above the wide tides of the Lough,
he strengthened and extended the old towers which dated from
King John's day, and made for himself "ane vera strong castle;
the lyk is not in the northe." He was created Viscount Clandeboye on May 4, 1622.

He was a most successful undertaker. From Scotland he
imported many families and many labourers to work his lands.
"They received," writes Cyril Falls of the Ulster plantation,
"a wilderness and made it a garden." His family affairs were

less successful. He married three times, but according to the Hamilton Manuscript, "his first two ladies proved but little comfortable to him." His eldest son, James Hamilton of Killyleagh, second Viscount Clandeboye, was created by Charles I Earl of Clanbrassil. Up to that moment things had gone remarkably well. Unfortunately Lord Clanbrassil's eldest son was a weakling and incapable of exercising his conjugal duties. He had married Lady Alice Moore, daughter of the first Earl of Drogheda "to the great grief of his mother and the trouble of all his relations." This lady, according to the Hamilton Manuscript, "soon appeared very high in her housekeeping and apparel and giving too much access to noblemen and gentlemen reputed vitious." She went further than that. As I have already recounted in *Helen's Tower* she burnt her father-in-law's will and then poisoned her weakling husband. A duplicate of the will was however discovered and the properties which the first James Hamilton had so intelligently amassed were split up among five of his nephews. As a result, the prosperity of the family was much dispersed. The castle of Killyleagh and the lands of Dufferin went to the eldest nephew, Gawen Hamilton, and through him they descended by an alternating succession of Gawens and Archibalds, until they eventually reached the Gawen Hamilton who was the father of Archibald Hamilton Rowan with whom this story deals.

(2)

In the drawing room at Killyleagh Castle there was a wide mantelpiece supported upon the upraised hands of cherubs. The cherubs in recent years have developed dry-rot and the mantelpiece has been changed. Above it, in my day, hung a conversation piece by Francis Wheatley, depicting Hamilton Rowan as a young man in the company of his mother and sister. The latter although very feminine in character, bore the virile name of Sydney. This picture must have been painted in or about 1777, that is a year before Francis Wheat-

ley eloped with Mrs. Gresse to Dublin, and three years before
Sydney, unable any longer to endure the bullying of her
mother, ran away with an elderly and impecunious clergyman
to Gretna Green. At the date of the picture Hamilton Rowan
was twenty-six and Sydney barely twelve.

This family group, ill composed but brightly coloured, gives
at first sight an amicable impression. It is only when one
examines it carefully that it becomes illustrative of the ten-
sion which warped three lives. Mrs. Gawen Hamilton is
seated in front of a colonnade opening upon a distant park. She
is heavily over-dressed and has puckered silk panniers round
her skirt; there is a turban on her head and she holds in her
hand what is probably a legal document, the contents of which
Hamilton Rowan is expounding to her with courteous em-
phasis. She gazes at her son with argumentative disapproval;
one can tell from the complacency of her pose, from the suspicious set of her eyes and mouth, from the sharp meanness
of her chin that she was a selfish woman with a touch of down-
right malice. Her daughter pauses timidly, aloof, hesitating
to descend the steps to the colonnade, and toying abstractedly
with a young spaniel. Hamilton Rowan himself stands there
as a patient colossus, and under the sleeve of his loose coat
one can detect the swell and weight of his enormous biceps.
Did I not know him so well I should suppose that there was
an ill-tempered, downward, look about his eyes and mouth.
He was not ill-tempered; he was the gayest, the friendliest,
of men. The expression which Wheatley has given to his
handsome features is one of respectful dislike. There must
have been moments when he hated his mother from the depths
of his unworldly soul.

The conjugal relations between Hamilton Rowan's father
and mother were never easy. Gawen Hamilton of Killyleagh
was not the type of husband likely either to attract or to control a woman of Mrs. Hamilton's ambitious temper. He was
a muddle-headed, untidy, raffish sort of man, liberal in his
sentiments, but possessing a taste for low company which in his

CONVERSATION PIECE BY FRANCIS WHEATLEY
HAMILTON ROWAN WITH HIS MOTHER AND SISTER

*See page 22*

THE KILLYLEAGH VOLUNTEERS DRILLING IN THE COURTYARD 1913

*See page 62*

later years became very marked indeed. When my mother was a girl he was still remembered at Killyleagh under the disrespectful name of "Old Baldie." He appears in fact to have been quite unwilling to maintain that position in society to which his estates entitled him and which his wife so ardently desired. He shambled through life untidily, quarrelling with his tenants, gazed at askance by the county families, and falling completely under the domination of his mistress, Ursula Carlisle, who began life as a housemaid at the Castle and ended by establishing a drunken domination over her ageing lover and the town of Killyleagh itself.

Mrs. Hamilton was of a different type. Although herself descended from a line of Scottish settlers in Ireland, although by family tradition belonging also to the protestant ascendancy, she had never become assimilated, she had never allowed the lure of Ireland to loosen the taut anglicanism of her mind. Her father, Mr. William Rowan, K.C., started his career as tutor to Lord George Sackville, and thereafter migrated to London, where he acquired a good legal practice, made a large fortune, and purchased several sites and properties in Marylebone, Hampstead and Highgate. His only child and sole heiress, Jane Rowan, married first Mr. Tichborne Aston of Co. Louth (by whom she had no children) and secondly Gawen Hamilton of Killyleagh. From the start she convinced herself that a woman of her capacity, an heiress to so large a fortune, would be wasted in the society of the squireens of Ballynahinch or Downpatrick, and that the proper setting for so rich a jewel was not the sea-weed of Strangford Lough but the parks and spas of London and the continent. From the first she decided that the child whom she had conceived at Killyleagh should be born and bred in England, and thus, a few weeks before his birth she left for ever the tumble-down castle of her husband and established herself in her father's house in Rathbone Place. It was here that, on May 12, 1751, Hamilton Rowan was born.

(3)

He was first sent as a day boarder to Mr. Fountain's school in Marylebone. He was happy enough with his school fellows and became a special favourite of the French master, Monsieur Morand, who would call him "mon petit Malebranche." The only quality in Hamilton Rowan which suggests any analogy with that distinguished metaphysician was his taste for argument; a taste which led Hamilton Rowan into many a disputation, and which caused Malebranche to fall dead with apoplexy after a short and perfectly amicable discussion with Bishop Berkeley. But in the evenings, when the sun began to slant down behind Tyburn Tree, it was necessary for the boy to return to Rathbone Place. That indeed was a constantly renewed ordeal. His mother would nag and fuss incessantly on the subject of deportment and clothes. It must be admitted that she was able to eradicate the Hamilton untidiness from his heredity, and he was always strikingly neat in his apparel and in his manners courteous and sedate. His grandfather, William Rowan, was definitely unkind. In later years Hamilton Rowan referred to the atmosphere of Rathbone Place with his usual placid generosity. "My grandfather," he wrote, "was of a choleric habit, while I was giddy and negligent, and therefore the time passed heavily enough." A contemporary passes a harsher judgment upon Mr. Rowan's treatment of young Hamilton Rowan. "Absolute nonsense," he wrote, "was his conduct of his grandson." This curious phrase implies something more eccentric and deliberate than the usual crustiness of an aged lawyer. It implies, on the part both of the grandfather and mother, a calculated system of coercive education. It implies that, in their folly, they believed that they could enucleate all Hamilton heredity, all trace of Irishness, from the boy's character. They failed.

I suspect Old Baldie of having been one of the major

causes of this failure. Hamilton Rowan's father was more than a whig; he was a radical. The atmosphere of Rathbone Place can never have been congenial to him and his presence in London was torture to Mrs. Hamilton's snobbish, possessive, soul. His sojourns in Ireland became more and more prolonged. On his return to London he would tell his boy stories about Killyleagh, about the horses and the sound of fishing smacks at dawn; about how the French under Thurot had landed that February at Kilroot point and seized the castle of Carrickfergus; about how Londonderry's handsome lad, young Robert Stewart, had almost been drowned in Strangford Lough; about the round holes in the tower parapets through which one could, if one so desired, pour molten lead upon one's enemies. Gawen Hamilton must frequently have been surprised to possess so tidy a son, even as the boy must have been disconcerted at having so untidy a father. But they loved each other dearly through all the troubles and disgraces of later life, and their joint dislike of Rathbone Place added an entrancing touch of confederacy to their relations.

Rathbone Place at that time was at the western edge of London abutting upon a large reservoir which worked a corn mill. The ground on either side of the reservoir had been turned into allotments tenanted by the Irish population of Soho. These people were, Hamilton Rowan records, "accustomed to spend the evenings in singing, dancing and other amusements of their country." How deeply Mr. Rowan and Mrs. Hamilton disapproved of these paddy ways!

From Mr. Fountain's seminary he went to Westminster. In order that the family discipline, the system devised by his grandfather and his mother, might vigilantly be continued a house was taken in the neighborhood of the school. Once again the boy was forced to alternate the discipline of the classroom with the even harsher discipline of his home life. He reacted against both.

There exists a vivid picture of Hamilton Rowan at this date, written by his former school-fellow Topham, then editor of the new and fashionable newspaper *The World*.

"With more than boyish aptitudes and abilities, his incessant intrepidity, his restless curiosity, his undertaking spirit,—all indicated early maturity. Hamilton was to be found in every daring oddity. Often has the morning caught him scaling the high pediments of the school door and clambering down opening the door within before the boy who kept the gate could come with the key. His evenings were set upon no less perils, with pranks and gunpowder, in leaping from unusual heights into the Thames.

"Through the intercourse of private life he is very amiable. The same suavity of speech, courteous attentions, and general good nature he had when a boy, are continued and improved. Good qualities the more to be prized, as less probable from his bold and eager temperament, from the turbulence of his wishes, and the hurry of his pursuits."

The discipline imposed upon him at home was of a nature at once to fortify his naturally rebellious instincts, and to deprive him of that self-reliance, that confidence in his immediate surroundings, from which soil alone a balanced habit can grow. The "turbulence of his wishes" must have enraged Mr. Rowan, even as the "hurry of his pursuits" must have jarred upon the careful calculating nature of his mother. In outward manner he was indeed becoming the cool foppish Englishman of her desires; but the impulsive Irishman raged underneath.

Even at Westminster there were certain elements which tugged him away from his conventional upbringing. Gawen Hamilton was known for his advanced opinions, and when the House of Commons rose at night some of the radical members would walk round to Cowley Street, drink large quantities of Mr. Hamilton's port, and discourse upon the dangers of the "new monarchy" of young George III and the iniquities of Bute and Grenville. The poet Churchill would be present at these meetings and speak with passion about his dear friend

Wilkes, about corruption in high places, about the coming dawn of English liberties. And there was Dr. Charles Lucas, the "first of Irish patriots," who also modelled himself, even in his manner of conversation, upon the genius of the "North Briton." Dr. Lucas, who was crippled with gout, would be wheeled into the dining room and would shake his silver locks in fury at the ruthlessness of the English administration in Ireland. Hamilton Rowan was much affected by Dr. Lucas. Here was a man who boasted of his English descent and of his Protestant convictions; here was a man who had defied the Lord Lieutenant and the whole Corporation of Dublin; here was a man who by his courageous attitude, by his espousal of the people's cause, had (in spite of social and physical disabilities) become the idol of the Irish mob. Here was a patriot, a martyr and a hero. Obstreperous and violent, fluent and vulgar, Dr. Lucas would raise his gouty fist in the Wilkes manner. What a relief were these intemperate outbursts from the tight-lipped disapproval, the prim silken rustle, of his mother's mode!

Mrs. Hamilton had evidently some suspicion that her son, however perfect might be his deportment, had inherited an undisciplined soul. She persuaded her father to make a will which would perpetuate the Rathbone Place system until he reached full age. Mr. Rowan died in 1767 when Hamilton Rowan was sixteen years old. Under his will he left his grandson the reversion of his entire fortune. The boy was at once to receive an annuity of £584; on attaining the age of twenty-five he was to be given a capital sum of £20,000; and on his mother's death he would inherit an annual income (irrespective of anything which he might derive from the Killyleagh estates) of more than £8,000 a year, representing some £20,000 a year in modern money. The legacy was, however, subjected to three important conditions:

(1) He was to assume the additional surname of Rowan.
(2) He was to take a degree either at Oxford or at Cambridge.

(3) He was not to visit Ireland before reaching the age of twenty-five.

The will contains a final paragraph illustrative of the spirit in which it was devised:

"I have made the foregoing device in favour of my said grandson, Archibald Hamilton Rowan, in the hope that he will prove an honest, learned and sober man, and live unbribed and unpensioned, loyal to his King and zealous for the rights of his country, and a true Protestant without bigotry to any sect or religion."

It cannot be contended that Hamilton Rowan in his subsequent life fulfilled all these hopes. He would have argued, in the Malebranche manner, that in using the phrase "his country" his grandfather had omitted to define whether England or Ireland was intended. But he could scarcely have argued that he ever displayed any loyalty at all to George III.

## (4)

The outward conditions which thus moulded his character and conduct, although conflicting, are obvious enough. The gift of caution, which he might well have derived from the Vicar of Dunlop, had been washed from his heredity by the soft tides of Strangford Lough. Although born and educated in England, yet his love of the unexpected rendered obnoxious to him the English pattern which his mother and grandfather sought to impose. As the years passed "England" became associated in his mind, not with the friendships of Westminster School nor yet with the frolics and opportunities of Cambridge, but with the meticulous routine, the constant carping, of Rathbone Place; whereas "Ireland" glimmered for him as a land of heroes and martyrs—of castles, battlements and fairies—as the land of the incalculable and the unexpected. London meant school-books and Mr. Rowan's ill temper and the irritated rustle of his mother's gown; Ireland signified the untamed and the rebellious. It possessed above all the glamour of a forbidden home. However delightful might seem the prospect of becoming an English country gentleman of elegance and fortune, such a future seemed unimaginative to his restless mind; *it was his mother's plan*. Hamilton Rowan always hated plans. How far more congenial, how far more suggestive of enterprise, were the uncalculated illusions, the gay good-tempered chuckles, of the father, their contempt for whom neither his mother nor his grandfather made any effort to conceal.

All this is explicable. Such elements, combining to affect an impetuous temperament, might be expected to produce an explosion. What is so strange about Hamilton Rowan's development is that this explosion was so long retarded, and that when it came it proved so ineffective. The story of his life, curious though it be, is not so very exceptional; what is exceptional is his constant inability to adjust his own impulsive opinions to the permanent ingredients of human nature; his astounding unawareness, that is, of the relation between thought and action, between the practical and the ideal.

It is here, and here only, that the really interesting problem occurs. Before giving the narrative of his adventures it will be well therefore to consider for a moment the eccentricity of temperament by which these adventures were produced. It is not what my great-great-grandfather did which perplexes me; I am used to aberrations of conduct; it is why he did it.

Dr. William Hamilton Drummond, who edited Hamilton Rowan's autobiography with really startling incompetence, was equally puzzled. He was so puzzled that he took the bust of Hamilton Rowan with him in a cab and drove to a phrenologist. The latter, having examined the bumps on the bust, reported as follows: "The most remarkable characteristic is love of approbation which is decidedly larger in proportion to the whole brain than in any other individual I have ever examined." "Combativeness," adds the phrenologist, "is very large. Cautiousness, acquisitiveness, secretiveness, veneration

—small." "A fondness for distinction," adds Dr. Hamilton Drummond on his own account, "formed a prominent feature in Mr. Hamilton Rowan's character." I cannot believe that vanity alone can bring a man to the very steps of the gallows. Was it his impetuosity which also contributed to disaster? I am reminded of Topham's references to his "love of bustle" and the "hurry of his pursuits." Hamilton Rowan was himself conscious of a certain unreasonable restlessness of habit. "I am," he confessed, "perpetually under weigh when I should have been at anchor." But mere restlessness does not involve a man in carefully contemplated plotting. Was it the romanticism of his age which upset his judgment? Even his contemporaries were perplexed. "It has often," writes one of them, "not only been lamented, but created wonder in many who knew him, how so much gentleness in private life could dwell in the frame of a man possessing so much public violence, sedition and treason." Was it quite simply that he was a stupid man? I do not think so. Drennan, writing to his brother-in-law on first meeting Hamilton Rowan in 1785 describes him as "a clever fellow who looks just the thing for a constitutional conspirator." Was it no more than a fatal capacity for imprudence? "Shall I ever act prudently?" he wrote to his wife, "probably never." Yet Hamilton Rowan was verging on middle age when he wrecked his own life and the lives of those he loved; and he had received ample and repeated warnings. Was it his passionate loyalty to his confederates who ill deserved such constancy? Sir Jonah Barrington, who after his own disgrace was apt to take a malicious delight in the disgrace of others, has not one word of unkindness to say about Hamilton Rowan. He speaks of his "unsophisticated patriotism." He speaks of "the spirit of false chivalry which took such entire possession of Hamilton Rowan's understanding." Even Jonah Barrington, a vivid psychologist, was nonplussed. Or was it that these defects—his love of approbation, his impulsiveness, his romanticism, his lack of caution, his jumbled loyalties—created an undergrowth of imprudence in which his feet became entangled? "Never," writes Charles Phillipps in *Curran and his Contemporaries,* "was there a man less capable of crime or more likely to commit an indiscretion." Yet such weaknesses, hampering though they may be to any practical success in life, do not usually lead to mistakes as gigantic as those committed by my great-great-grandfather. His really deplorable career is best explained by examining the chain of circumstances which led him, link by link, to his final catastrophe. But even when we have scrutinized each link, and appraised the chain as a whole we shall be left with the final interrogative—"Why? Why? Why?"

The problem remains.

# II

## YOUTH, 1767–1780

Cambridge–A visit to Holland–The Huntingdon Militia–Martha Ray–Visit to America–Charleston in 1771–Hounslow Heath–Crosses to France–French enlightenment and the Freemasons–At Rouen–Visit to Portugal–Meets Marie Antoinette–George Robert Fitzgerald–A disreputable duel–Meeting with Benjamin Franklin–Early disloyalties to the English Government.

### (1)

AFTER leaving Westminster School Hamilton Rowan came to adopt quite naturally the habits of life then expected of a young Englishman of independent means. He matriculated at Queen's College, Cambridge, and he spent his first vacation, in the company of his friend Sir John Borlase Warren, on a skating expedition in Holland. His career at Cambridge was, it is true, not unmarked by a certain recklessness of temper. He climbed up all the sign-posts in the neighbourhood and changed the indicators the wrong way round. He threw his tutor into the Cam. He lived in jovial company and in spite of his large income he contracted heavy debts. "While at Cambridge," writes Dr. Hamilton Drummond, "he and several of his fellow students were in the habit of meeting in each other's chambers and of indulging in rude and boisterous mirth. On one of these occasions they indulged in a rough sport which led them to throw the furniture out of the windows, part of which fell on a gentleman's coach passing at the time." For these and other offences he was rusticated by the college authorities and spent a penitential year with Dr. Enfield at the Warrington Academy. He was permitted to return to

Cambridge to take his degree, thereby fulfilling one of the three provisions of his grandfather's will. He did not, however, abide by the provision which enjoined him never to visit Ireland until he reached the age of twenty-five. On more than one occasion, he confesses, he sneaked clandestinely to Killyleagh.

While still at Cambridge Hamilton Rowan was given by the Duke of Manchester a commission in the Huntingdon Militia. "From the time," he writes, "that I first mounted my epaulettes, I paid but little attention either to college rules or exercises, and merely kept the necessary terms." While thus engaged he formed a friendship with Lord Charles Montagu who often took him to visit Lord Sandwich at Hinchingbrooke. It was there that he met the celebrated singer Martha Ray, mistress to Lord Sandwich, who after dinner would entertain the company with pretty songs. "At these performances," writes Hamilton Rowan, "the company invited by his Lordship would retire with him. His servant then brought in tumblers of negus, and plates of thin slices of bread and butter with cold meat between each, and presented them to the spectators." Among those who shared this collation, which has added a familiar word to our language, was the Rev. James Hackman, who became so desperately enamoured of Miss Ray that he finally shot her in the head outside Covent Garden Theatre upon April 7, 1779. On his journey to Tyburn Hackman was accompanied in the mourning coach by James Boswell, who dined out upon the episode that evening, and has recorded the fierce altercation which arose around it between Topham Beauclerk and Dr. Johnson.

Lord Charles Montagu was at the time Governor of South Carolina and was ordered by Lord North to return to his post from which he had been absent upon indefinite leave. He and Lady Charles drove down to Falmouth with a numerous retinue including Hamilton Rowan. The frigate *Tartar*, Captain Meadows, was waiting to take them to

America and at the last moment Hamilton Rowan decided, since "there was still a good part of the long vacation to spare," to accompany them.    It was a rough voyage and Lady Charles suffered so much from sea-sickness that Captain Meadows was obliged to put in at the Azores.    On arriving at Charleston, Hamilton Rowan was impressed by the fact that "the bickerings between England and the Colonies were becoming serious."    The Assembly of South Carolina had just voted a sum of £45 for repainting the railings around the statue of the elder Pitt which still stands there in front of the court-house.    Lord Charles decided that this act represented a studied insult to Lord North and dissolved the Assembly.    Writs were issued for a new election but identically the same members were returned.    The reconstituted Assembly again passed a vote of £45 for repainting the railings round the statue of the elder Pitt.    Lord Charles was incensed by such subordination.    He sent his officer down to the Assembly, accompanied by a drummer, with instructions to dissolve the Assembly a second time.    The members shut themselves up in the Assembly Hall, bolted and barred the doors, and passed the offending measure.    They then opened the doors, allowed the drummer to enter, and were again dissolved.    Lord Charles felt himself obliged to refuse to sanction the bill about the railings, but since the members had had the sense to tie it up to the current vote of Credit, the whole year's expenditure of the Colony was left unprovided.    The bickerings continued.

After remaining three months at Charleston, and since the sands of the long vacation were running very low, Hamilton Rowan decided that it was time to return to Cambridge.    He brought home with him a racoon, an opossum and a young bear.    Each of these three animals died, or was washed overboard, during the journey.    Such was his first, but not his last, visit to America.

He returned to England, took his degree, and established himself in London.    At the same time he kept a large stable at Bedfont near Hounslow Heath under the charge of a reputed highwayman of the name of "Sixteen String Jack." He would often notice in the morning that some of his best horses had had a night out. Throughout this period he was recklessly extravagant, and indeed he seems never to have appreciated the difference between capital and income or to have possessed even a rudimentary talent for accounts. He was obliged to have recourse to a convivial but fraudulent solicitor of the name of Greenway who encouraged him to draw many bills upon the money which would be his on reaching the age of twenty-five. By this means he was able to pay off his creditors and was left with a large sum of ready cash in hand. He decided none the less to leave England. He sold his house and stable and crossed to France. This was in the year 1773 when he was twenty-two years old.

## (2)

The pages of his autobiography and the records of his contemporaries furnish no explanation why, at this stage of his life, Hamilton Rowan chose to retire to the continent. With but infrequent visits to England he remained there for eleven years. He could not have left England in order to escape from his creditors since he expressly states that they had all been paid. The whole habits of his life, his love of dogs and rowing, his affection for his school and college friends, should have tempted him to remain in England and to have enjoyed the many amenities of London or Newmarket. I suspected at one time that he must have fled from England in order to escape from his mother's incessant bullying, but here again there is no evidence to suggest such unfilial behaviour. When he visited London he lived quite amicably with his mother, either at Pinner or in Great Marlborough Street. The Francis Wheatley conversation piece itself attests that there was no open quarrel. I can only imagine that some unfortunate love affair drove him from his home, and that thereafter he became attached to the continental way of life. But for this there is no circumstantial evidence at all.

When I examine the chain of circumstance which led him to Newgate Prison I am bound to admit that at this part of the chain there are several links missing. I do not know why he left England. I do not know why, after four years' residence in France, he began to adopt an anti-English attitude. It is certain only that during those four years between 1773 and 1777 something important happened in his mind. What was that something?

There are three main types of revolutionary. There is the patriot type, such as Masaryk or De Valera, whose central purpose is the liberation of their country from foreign rule. There is the doctrinaire type, such as Robespierre or Lenin, whose aim is to impose by force upon their fellow men some social or economic theory in which they fanatically believe. And there is the opportunist type, such as Napoleon or Hitler, who, while adopting the phraseology of revolution, seek to find in revolutionary disturbance opportunity for their personal ambition. Between these three main types are several intermediate types of lesser men. These types, in their turn, fall into recognizable categories. There is the intellectual theorist who imagines that the ills of this world are the result, not of the eternal defects of human nature, but of remedial faults in existing conditions or institutions. There is the egoist who ascribes to his environment that lack of personal success which is in fact due to his own deficiency in mental or moral vigour. There is the disappointed or unadaptable man who has a grievance against society to which he ascribes the misfortunes or hostility which, owing to his own regrettable character, he has encountered. And there is the thoughtless optimist who, without study or application, believes that if he drifts in the tide of "progress" he will have the right to call himself "progressive."

Hamilton Rowan does not fall comfortably into any of these categories. He was not a patriot, in the sense that he had no nationalist emotions and cared more for the rights of man than for the rights of Ireland. He was not a profound ideologist, since he would have been unable to formulate his ideology in any but the most superficial terms. He had no personal ambition, beyond the vain desire for esteem. He was not an intellectual, nor did he possess any deep or constant interest in the intellectual ferment of his time. Nor was he in any ascertainable sense a disappointed man. I quite see that he lacked all conception of the relation between aims and their results; I quite see that he transferred his sentiments into objective realities, until reality itself became transfigured. I quite see that such expressions as "tyranny," "aristocracy," "sovereign people" or "natural man" became for him during those years a series of incantations which he believed to be rational. I quite see that, having adopted as his religion a doctrine which he soon saw to be a fallacy he was too conceited to admit that he was wrong. I see even that when, at a later date, he discovered that his fellow believers in "the sovereign people" were in fact aiming at depriving others of privilege in order to enjoy privilege themselves, he resolved to prove by self-sacrifice that he at least was disinterested and incorruptible. I see all this. I can identify all these emotions. They were at that date not in the least exceptional emotions; they were common emotions; they were even fashionable. They induced in many of his contemporaries a disastrous lack of faith in their own formula; they destroyed in the ruling classes of France the very desire for dominion. They created a transitory mood of internationalism, a temporary suspension of patriotism. But they did not combine to create the central fire of rebellion. It is the position of that central flame which, in Hamilton Rowan, it is so difficult to locate.

The temperament of a quisling can readily be recognized. It is composed of frustrated egoism, and in the youth of a quisling it is generally possible to find some ill-adjustment to environment, some early incident by which the rewards of

intelligence and vigour were denied. Hamilton Rowan un-
doubtedly possessed some of the quisling characteristics; he
was vain, impatient, impetuous and reckless to a degree. But
I cannot trace in his early life any of these frustrations, en-
mities or disappointments which give to quislings their minority
feelings. His was a gay and amicable nature; even in his most
seditious days he displayed none of that rancour which leads
men to plot against their environment. He had been accorded
exceptional opportunities in worldly life; a future of ease and
happiness seemed to open before him. He was not by nature
a political animal, nor can I understand why he left the easy
orbit of his interests and capacities, to embark upon transactions
far beyond his depth.

It is tempting to attribute his change of heart and mind to
the supposition that after a few months' residence in France
he became intoxicated by the wave of enlightenment which
was sweeping the French governing classes to their own destruction. He probably read Voltaire and Montesquieu but
it may be doubted whether their eulogy of English institutions made any deep impression on his mind. He must certainly have read *La Nouvelle Héloise and Emile* and it is clear
that the phraseology of the *Contrat Social,* with all those
facile assumptions regarding the natural rights of man and
the infallibility of the general will, became part of the furniture of his brain. But he was not a deep reader, nor was
his temperament attuned to the nervous sensibility of Jean
Jacques Rousseau. There is small trace in his letters and comments at the time, either of any deep spirit of criticism of the
existing French system, or of the philosophic jargon of the
Paris salons. Unquestionably he absorbed a large proportion
of the "discontent with civilization" which was in the air. Unquestionably he shared the then fashionable illusion that "reason" was omnipotent and infallible and that "man" had merely
to be "freed" from existing institutions to regain his pristine
wisdom and purity of soul. Unquestionably he convinced
himself that the faults of society could be directly attributed

to the oppression of the governing classes and that with the removal of privilege these faults, as if by magic, would melt away. What is difficult to understand is under what influence or impulse Hamilton Rowan was driven to translate these fashionable sympathies into personal action of so extreme a form. Many thoughtless men are driven by conceit or obstinacy into an exaggerated expression of their own chance opinions; but in almost every case in which such obstinacy is translated into dangerous action one can find some internal or external explanation to account for such conduct. In Hamilton Rowan I can find neither an external nor an internal cause.

It may be, of course, that he was led into conspiracy by the French freemasons. He had himself been initiated when an Undergraduate and had in fact become Master of the Cambridge Lodge. The Grand Orient, with Philippe Egalité as its Grand Master, was founded in Paris in 1772 with the slogan "Liberty and Equality." The term "fraternity" was added to the slogan later by the Martinists. It may be even that he met Adam Weishaupt, who had a predilection for handsome young men of good family and "high soulful eyes," and that he was enrolled among the "Illuminati." I can quite imagine Hamilton Rowan, whose curiosity was of the rambling type, becoming interested in occultism and in the mysteries of the Cabala. But if this be true then it is strange that there should be no trace in any of his writings or correspondence of the mumbo-jumbo in which the Illuminati indulged. He did not call himself an "areopagist" nor did he address his friends by cryptic names such as "Paulonius" or "Agathon." He was a freemason certainly; but there is no cause to suspect that he was a member of the more secretive or more anarchistic wings.

The facts which he gives us of his sojourn in France are ordinary and vague. He spent almost two years at Rouen, where he made friends with Count O'Rourke, an Irish refugee, and with a Mr. Holker, who had fled his country after the

events of 1745 and established a lucrative cotton manufactory
in France. From Rouen he went to Paris, where he settled
for several years. Apart from his occasional visits to London or Pinner he remained in France. In the autumn of
1777 he did, it is true, undertake a curious and abortive journey to Portugal. King Joseph's favourite, the Marquess de
Pombal, had conceived the idea of enlisting British officers
for the Portuguese army. Lord Charles Montagu persuaded Hamilton Rowan that, if he accompanied him to Lisbon he would at once be appointed a Portuguese colonel.
On their arrival, however, they discovered that Pombal had
fallen and they were obliged to return. Hamilton Rowan
came back via Gibraltar, Tangier and Port Mahon. From
Marseilles he drove to Paris. There are three incidents which
occurred during this sojourn in Paris which throw a side-
light upon his character. The first was connected with Marie
Antoinette, the second with George Robert Fitzgerald and
the third with Benjamin Franklin. These incidents are worth
recording.

(3)

In order to amuse himself while in Paris he had written to
Messrs. Roberts of Lambeth asking them to send him one of
the Thames wherries such as he used to hire when a boy at
Westminster School. The boat arrived and Hamilton Rowan,
who was an expert oarsman, spent many happy hours rowing
upon the Seine. One day he learned that Marie Antoinette
would proceed by water to Fontainebleau accompanied by a
numerous retinue. He decided to join the procession in his
little boat. "I imagined," he records, "that I possessed superior dexterity in its management and this led me to accompany
the cortège. My boat was taken notice of for I saw the Queen
speaking to the Duc de Lauzun and pointing it out. But alas,
when I asked him what she had said, he told me that the only
remark she had made was, "Que cela peut être amusement
pour un seigneur anglois!" It would seem that Marie An-

toinette did in fact pay some attention to the gigantic Englishman in the little boat. She sent him a ring in token of the
occasion, a ring which today is still preserved in the family.

The second incident is less comprehensible. Visiting Paris
at that time was an Irishman of the name of George Robert Fitzgerald, a descendant of the Desmond branch of the
Geraldine family, known by the frequency of his duels as
"Fighting Fitzgerald." He retained throughout his life the
milk-white complexion, and the boyish soprano voice, which
had rendered him so conspicuous when at Eton. As a duel-
list he bore an unsavoury reputation and his social position
had further been disturbed by the fact that he had been prosecuted in the Irish courts for abducting his younger brother,
and for harnessing his aged father to a dray in Co. Mayo.
Hamilton Rowan's first contact with Fitzgerald was inauspi-
cious, the latter having given him a stumer cheque in purchase of a horse. One evening, however, on leaving the
Comédie Italienne, Hamilton Rowan observed an altercation
taking place in the lobby. A Major Baggs, who was owed
£300 by Fitzgerald, had the impudence, on meeting him at
the exit to the opera, to remind him of the fact. Fitzgerald
struck him across the face with his glove and a scuffle ensued.
The combatants were parted and Fitzgerald then asked Hamilton Rowan to act as his second in the inevitable duel. It is
difficult for us today to understand, or to be interested in,
the etiquette of these affairs of honour. In Ireland duelling
had for long been an established practice. The Lord Chancellor (Lord Clare) had fought a duel with the Master of
the Rolls (Mr. Curran). The Chief Justice, Lord Clonmell, fought four duels. The Chancellor of the Exchequer
had fought Mr. Grattan and the Provost of the University
of Dublin had gone all the way to Minden to fight with
Mr. Doyle. Yet in spite of the high repute in which duelling was held at the time, it is difficult to see what obligation of honour, except his own reckless loyalty, can have imposed upon Hamilton Rowan the necessity of acting as second

to a man whom he much disliked, whose duelling reputation was most unsavoury, and in a quarrel in which the right was wholly upon the other side. His intervention in the affair was bound to involve him in scandal, in much personal inconvenience, and even in some personal danger, since the French edicts against duelling were at the time severe. Yet his curious sense of honour, his fantastic loyalty, forced him to become involved. As might well have been foreseen, the incident did not redound to Fitzgerald's credit or to that of his second.

In order to avoid the penalties of French law the duel had to take place beyond Valenciennes, in the Austrian Netherlands. Fitzgerald wounded Major Baggs at the first discharge of his pistol and then fired a second shot at him while lying upon the ground. Hamilton Rowan protested to Fitzgerald against this unseemly action but the latter merely replied, "I would not have done it to any man but Baggs." Thereafter Fitzgerald escaped to Brussels, returned to Ireland and was subsequently hanged at Castlebar for the murder of a soldier. Before he departed he induced Hamilton Rowan to cash a further stumer cheque. The latter thereafter had to face the trouble alone. He was sent for by the Governor of Valenciennes and told that instructions had been received that he should be despatched under police escort to Paris. As, however, the Governor observed a jewelled masonic badge dangling from Hamilton Rowan's watch-chain he was content to accept his word of honour that on his return to Paris he would report himself to the Hôtel de Montmorenci. He did so; and was molested no further.

The American War of Independence had by then broken out and the French and British Governments were officially and actually at war. This did not, however, in those easygoing days, affect civilian intercourse between the two countries. English visitors still flocked to Paris, the only restriction being that they were obliged to cross by Ostend instead of by Calais. Hamilton Rowan, in spite of his commission in the Huntingdon Militia, remained on in Paris, rowing his wherry peacefully upon the Seine. Meanwhile Benjamin Franklin had arrived as representative of the thirteen colonies. Hamilton Rowan asked for an audience and was gracefully received, "which," he records, "I esteemed no small honour." He went further. He used his acquaintance with Benjamin Franklin to enlist Englishmen in the American forces for the purpose of fighting against their own country. The incident is best recorded in his own ingenuous words. "I received," he writes in his Autobiography, "a visit from an old friend, who had the rank of lieutenant-colonel in the British Army, accompanied by a lieutenant of a man-of-war, of old standing but without interest, and of course without hope of promotion. Their object was to obtain commissions in the American army and navy; they applied to me to introduce them to Dr. Franklin. The Doctor received them politely; but said he was not authorized to make any military appointments; yet was certain that every attention would be paid to them, should they go to America. This was a risk they did not choose to venture; and some years after, the one died commanding a regiment of loyal Americans, who were to serve only in the islands; and the other a commodore in the British navy."

It is difficult to fix the date of this strange episode, which Hamilton Rowan slips so innocently into his autobiographical notes. He was as incapable of exact chronology as he was incapable of exact finance, and some of his stories are manifestly recorded in the wrong order. We know that Benjamin Franklin arrived in Paris in December 1776 and there is strong reason to suppose that Hamilton Rowan was in London in June 1777. It is probable that his attempt to recruit senior officers for service with our enemies was made in the spring of 1777, that is four years after he had arrived in France and seven years before he settled in Ireland. It is clear therefore that it was not the wrongs of Ireland alone which turned him against the country of his birth and up-bringing.

Meanwhile he still retained the King's commission and from time to time he would cross to England to visit his mother and little sister. In a book published in 1789, and entitled *Biographical anecdotes of the founders of the Irish Rebellion*, there is a convincing picture of Hamilton Rowan during one of these visits. He returned, it is recorded, "with all the frippery of dress which at that time distinguished the beaux of Paris." He was in fact laughed at by two footmen in St. James's Park, who, "little imagining the muscular strength which was cloathed with so much effeminacy, received from Mr. Hamilton Rowan upon the instant each a severe drubbing for their insolence." Whereafter, we may suppose, he returned to Great Marlborough Street and to the orderly social world through which his mother, clothed in bronze or purple silk, sailed like a galleon, with his small sister in tow behind.

# III

## THE BERESFORD CASE, 1780–1784

His sister Sydney–Her elopement with the Rev. Benjamin Beresford–Gretna Green–Mrs. Hamilton appeals to the Lord Chancellor–Sydney confined in an asylum at Lille–The *lettre de cachet*–
The case before the Parlement of Paris–The judgment reversed by
royal decree–Hamilton Rowan marries Sarah Dawson–His letters
to her–The Petit Hôtel de Choiseul–Effect upon him of his first
sojourn in Paris–His regrettable reticence and lack of observation–
His autobiography–Its faults and omissons–The shallow temperament–Establishes himself in Ireland.

## (1)

THERE occurred at this time an incident which caused public
scandal both in England and France and which did damage
to the social position which Mrs. Hamilton had so assiduously
cultivated.

In addition to her London house in Great Marlborough
Street she possessed a country house at Pinner, to which she
would retire when fashion waned. She came to know the
Vicar of Pinner and not infrequently would honour the
Vicarage with her presence. On one such visit she met the
Reverend Benjamin Beresford, chaplain to the Duke of Bedford, who would occasionally come down to Pinner and preach
a sermon at the village church. Mr. Beresford was a man
of some thirty-five years of age. It was assumed by his friends
that a cleric of his gifts, good manners, intelligence, and powerful connections would have a successful career in the Church
and might with confidence aspire to an Irish bishopric. Mrs.
Hamilton, who was of a patronizing temperament, had re-

cently admitted into her family circle a Miss Sarah Dawson, the daughter of a former Irish neighbour—a girl of ro-
bust but prepossessing appearance, strong character and no
fortune.   Mrs. Hamilton conceived the idea that the Reverend Beresford would make an admirable husband for Sarah
Dawson and invited him to the house.   He came there frequently.

Miss Sydney Hamilton, at that date, was fifteen years of
age.   Shy, timorous, ill-educated but packed with sensibility,
she yearned to escape from her mother's domination.   The
latter, it is evident, ill-treated the child and it was stated in
evidence that she actually beat her.   The affection lavished
by Mrs. Hamilton upon Miss Sarah Dawson, the comparisons
which she drew between the competence of this dependent
and the wistful inefficiency of her own daughter, filled Sydney with jealousy and rage.   Her only confidant was Letitia
Sutcliffe, personal maid to Mrs. Hamilton, and by coincidence
the clandestine wife of Henry Dally, man-servant to the Reverend Benjamin Beresford.   Letitia Sutcliffe encouraged the
emotions of resentment and frustration which seethed in Sydney's mind.   She went further.   She implied to Sydney that
the Reverend Benjamin Beresford was stricken by her charms,
and through Henry Dally she instilled into the clergyman
stories of the indignities to which the poor girl was constantly exposed.   Romance flowered.   It does not seem that
the child held much open converse with Mr. Beresford, but
it was noticed that his visits to Pinner, and the sermons which
he there delivered, became more frequent and more studied.   Sydney would sit there in the pew gazing up at her
clergyman displaying strength and gentleness from the pulpit.
And thus, on the night of November 1, 1780, the elopement
occurred.

Sydney, that evening, had pleaded a headache and retired
early to bed.   Sarah Dawson, who shared her room, followed later.   In order to reach or leave their room the girls
had to pass through that of Mrs. Hamilton.   That evening,

however, the mother remained downstairs till midnight, attending to her correspondence.  So soon as Sarah Dawson fell asleep, Sydney Hamilton (who had slipped into her bed fully dressed) crept out silently, pulled the curtains of the bed tight behind her, and arranged upon the chair beside it a heap of discarded clothes.  Her mother, on retiring to rest, looked into the girls' room, heard the sound breathing of Sarah Dawson, noticed the drawn curtains of her daughter's bed and the pile of clothes beside it, and satisfied herself that all was well.  Sydney by then had already taken refuge in Letitia Sutcliffe's room preparing her escape.  When all was quiet, Sydney and Letitia crept down the stairs to the back door.  The noise roused Mrs. Hamilton who rang her bell. It was answered after some interval, not by Letitia, but by the cook.  Mrs. Hamilton told her that she had heard noises and enquired whether all the doors were locked.  By that time, however, Sydney and Letitia had already reached the Queen's Head at Pinner where they found waiting for them, the Reverend Benjamin Beresford, Henry Dally and a postchaise.  They drove with speed to Gretna Green and were married by the blacksmith.

Next morning Mrs. Hamilton discovered her daughter's disappearance and immediately ordered her carriage to be prepared.  The coachman (and this is significant of the sympathy which Sydney's plight had aroused in the household) refused to obey this order.  An express was sent off to Hamilton Rowan, who happened to be in England and to be staying in Lincolnshire.  He also displayed unwillingness to intervene.  Mrs. Hamilton then hurried to London and interviewed her lawyers.  They advised her to petition the Lord Chancellor for an injunction and prepared a deposition for her to sign.  In this deposition she was at pains to rebut in advance any suggestion that she had in fact ill-treated her daughter.  She claims that "without rigidness" she had sought to instil into Sydney's mind the "principles of Duty, Virtue and Honour."  She adds that she had herself told the girl that if she contracted a marriage suitable to her station she would be allowed a settlement of £30,000. She contends that so large a dowry entitled both her daughter and herself to anticipate a "most respectable connection." With this in mind Mrs. Hamilton had "endeavoured to bestow upon her a polite education and had for that purpose placed her in one of the first Boarding Schools in the Kingdom." Sydney had been unhappy at school and had returned to Pinner where she had been provided with a music master, a dancing master, a drawing master "and a gentleman to instruct her in reading." Mrs. Hamilton admitted that the girl had never been allowed out alone, that she had always slept in a room adjoining her mother, and that she had been kept under watchful discipline. On the other hand she had accompanied her mother to places of entertainment, had "taken the Air with her in her carriage," and had on one occasion, for her delectation, been accompanied to Margate. By these precautions Mrs. Hamilton hoped that she had "secured her against any attempts that might be made to allure, seduce or convey her away."

Then came Mr. Beresford, chaplain to the Duke of Bedford. "The Deponent was thus induced," runs the deposition, "to receive the said Benjamin Beresford in a polite manner and to enter into conversation with him." In fact the Rev. Gentleman came often to their house, "loitering there and using every Art to make himself agreeable and entertaining, without in the least appearing to pay any attention to Miss Hamilton." On the contrary, his affections appeared to centre upon Miss Dawson "with whom he had danced at an assembly at Stanmore and whom he seemed to admire." Yet all the time he had been in secret communication with Miss Hamilton through Letitia Sutcliffe "by whose means the Deponent's daughter was betrayed, seduced and conveyed away and put into possession of the said Benjamin Beresford" with the result that "the said Benjamin Beresford and the said Sydney Hamilton had been joined together in matrimony at a place called Gretna Green on the borders of Scotland."

(2)

Had the story ended there, it might be possible to feel that Mrs. Hamilton was justified in her fury and that the Rev. Beresford had in fact conspired with Mr. and Mrs. Dally to abduct the foolish child and to profit by her fortune. I should not have felt this myself, partly because of the Francis Wheatley picture and the horrible description it gives of Mrs. Hamilton's character, and partly because I should have found it difficult to believe that a man of Mr. Beresford's age and education could for one moment have imagined that such an elopement was likely to bring him either Hamilton money or church advancement. But the story did *not* end there. It continued for some years to weave a curious pattern in the lives of these four people. The immediate sequel was that Mrs. Hamilton behaved with such stratagem and malice that she was fined the sum of £50,000 by the Parlement of Paris. The ultimate sequel was that Hamilton Rowan, impressed by the good sense manifested throughout the ensuing troubles by Sarah Dawson, fell in love with her, and remained in love with her all his life. And the Beresfords, after many months of bitterness and separation, were finally reunited and lived happily ever afterwards. Their son, a gifted young man, eventually married his first cousin, Hamilton Rowan's daughter, much to the contentment of all concerned.

The immediate sequel was, however, harrowing in the extreme. I should never have heard of this sequel had not my cousin, Hans Rowan Hamilton, in his researches into the history of his family, discovered a book in Paris entitled *Histoire de Miss Sydney Hamilton*. The book is dated 1785 and was published in a series of *Causes Célèbres* by "Mérigot jeune, Libraire, Quai des Augustins, au coin de la rue pavée." From this book, which my cousin has generously placed at my disposal, I have been able to reconstruct the bitter struggle which ensued.

The Rev. Beresford, on his return from Gretna Green, heard of the injunction applied for to the Lord Chancellor and realized that he was in a dangerous position, having abducted a child below the age of consent. He hid his young wife in a dress-maker's establishment at Marylebone, published the bans in an obscure church, and married her again on December 11 in accordance with English law. He then took her to live with him in a house in Duke Street. They were without any means of subsistence, since the Duke of Bedford had felt bound to part with his chaplain, and Sydney was in the end obliged to enter into communication with her mother and to beg for forgiveness. Her mother replied in a short unsigned note as follows:

"That I tenderly loved my daughter is past doubt.
That she equally was most dear to her brother is most certain,
That I will avenge the injury done her is most sure.
That I will never again see her is most sure."

In despair, Sydney burst into her mother's house in Great Marlborough Street and a reconciliation was effected on certain conditions. Sydney must refuse to have any further communication with her husband and must agree to leave immediately for abroad. Meanwhile Mrs. Hamilton consulted her lawyers as to the best means of prosecuting the Rev. Beresford, but they insisted that she could only do so with Gawen Hamilton's consent. Old Baldie refused for several months to give this consent and meanwhile Sydney confessed that she was with child. Mrs. Hamilton thereupon packed her off to Lille and arranged that she should be confined in a lunatic asylum. She remained there for five months. No money was allowed her and she was obliged to pawn her clothes. Meanwhile the Rev. Beresford obtained from the Lord Chancellor, Lord Mansfield, a *habeas corpus* enjoining Mrs. Hamilton to produce his wife. Alarmed by this threat Mrs.

Hamilton in her turn escaped to the continent, and took an apartment at Lille where Sydney joined her. The distracted Mr. Beresford managed to ascertain their place of hiding, journeyed to Lille and applied to the local court for the restitution of his wife. Accompanied by two of the Lille sheriffs Mr. Beresford entered the apartment in which Mrs. Hamilton and her daughter were then staying and, in the presence of two English witnesses, induced the latter to sign a paper stating that she loved her husband and was anxious to resume her married life. This paper was attested by the Court of Lille but Mrs. Hamilton appealed against this decision to the higher Court at Douai. The decision was confirmed. In the midst of these agitations Sydney, on August 10, gave birth to a daughter. Mrs. Hamilton covered her head in shame and refused even to glance at the infant. She had it registered as "the child of parents whose marriage is contested."

Mrs. Hamilton appears, at that date, to have possessed influential friends at Versailles. Through them she appealed to Louis XVI and obtained from him a *lettre de cachet* by which Mr. Beresford was removed under arrest to Paris. By that time moreover she had extracted from Old Baldie a power of attorney empowering her to act on his behalf. Thus armed she journeyed with her daughter to Paris and instituted proceedings against Mr. Beresford for abduction and *mésalliance*. Mr. Beresford, who had managed to interest the Parlement of Paris in his case, countered with an order placing Mrs. Hamilton and his wife under police supervision. The case was heard before the Chamber of Tournelle of the Paris Parlement in March 1782. The court was presided over by the Advocate General d'Aguesseau, grandson of the famous chancellor. M. de Limon acted as counsel for Mrs. Hamilton; the Reverend Beresford was defended by Monsieur Target; and MM. Elie de Beaumont and Lacretelle held watching briefs for Sydney and her infant. The case attracted much attention since it was regarded as a test battle between the

Parlement and Versailles. "An immense concourse of people of all ranks," records the *Mercure de France*, "attended the court, being attracted by the singularity of the matter and the lively interest which it inspired."

Monsieur de Limon opened his case for Mrs. Hamilton by emphasizing the difference in rank between Sydney Hamilton and the Reverend Benjamin Beresford. Sydney, according to M. de Limon, was descended not merely from the Earls of Clanbrassil, not only from the Dukes of Hamilton, but also from Henri I of France and all the kings of Scotland. Mr. Beresford on the other hand was the son of a cobbler of Bewdley and had started life as a grocer's assistant. Mrs. Hamilton, he went on to explain, was a stern but tender mother, imbued with the principles of Locke, "dédaignant les talens agréables (peu communs en Angleterre) et mettant peut-être, car il faut tout avouer, une nuance de trop de gravité et d'uniformité." He then went on to describe the sinister plot which the Reverend Beresford with the assistance of Henry Dally and Letitia Sutcliffe had hatched against the child Sydney. "On n'envisage pas," he said, "sans frémir d'horreur, la trame infernale qu'il a ourdie." He made quite a good point in stating that Mr. Beresford had first seen his victim when preaching to her from the pulpit, "du haut de la chaire de Vérité." He went on to describe in lurid detail the manoeuvres by which Mr. Beresford, "ce prêtre profanateur de son ministère," had engineered the elopement; he slid over the lunatic asylum at Lille by referring to it as "l'obscurité profonde d'une retraite obscure": and he ended by a passionate appeal begging the Advocate General not to accord approval in France to crimes committed in England or to hand over to such a scoundrel the innocent victim who had been snatched from her mother's arms.

M. Target, for Beresford, emphasized the ill treatment from which Sydney had suffered at the hands of her mother; drew attention to the delicacy of Beresford in regularizing the Gretna Green marriage by a subsequent marriage at "Duck Street, Sainte Marie la Bonne"; referred to the asylum at Lille in which Mrs. Hamilton had incarcerated her daughter as a place "réservée à la démence et la pauvreté"; pointed out that the charge of "mésalliance" did not exist in English law; and appealed to the magistrate to remember that the sacred laws of marriage and the needs of justice were higher things than any lineage or any powerful connections. His peroration was superb. Pointing a finger at Mrs. Hamilton, as she sat there arrayed in bronze silk, he addressed her as "Cruelle et implacable ennemie." "Here you have," he exclaimed, "a mother escaping from British law in the hope of invoking French law against her own daughter, in the hope of profiting by the blind obedience of a little child in order to condemn this child to the disgrace of adultery and to brand upon the forehead of her speechless infant the name of bastard."

The Parlement of Paris felt that here was an occasion to display their own integrity and their historic independence; to deal one more blow at the tottering fabric of Versailles; to demonstrate that, even in war time, the spirit of justice still glowed with undimmed fire at the Châtelet; to make a popular gesture in the cause of equality and the rights of man; to annoy the King; to humiliate the King's favourites; and to establish the rights of the middle classes against the aristocracy. They therefore gave judgment against Mrs. Hamilton. They decreed that Beresford should at once be released; that Mrs. Hamilton should pay him damages to the amount of £50,000 for unwarranted arrest, this sum to be held in trust for Sydney's infant; that she should pay all the costs of the case; and that all parties should be sent back to England there to settle according to English law the legality of the marriage. Mrs. Hamilton's fury knew no bounds. She exercised all the influence of which she was capable; she pulled every string; and a month later the decision of the Parlement of Paris was reversed by a royal decree which ran as follows:

"Given in the King's Council of State, His Majesty being there present, held at Versailles on April 27, 1782. The King having had exhibited to him in Council the decrees of the Parlement of Paris of the 25th of last March in the suit depending between Mr. Benjamin Beresford on the one part and Mr. and Mrs. Hamilton and their daughter on the other, has decided to vacate and annul the decisions of the Parlement in the Châtelet in Paris as in all other tribunals in his kingdom. He orders that the guards on Miss Hamilton be withdrawn immediately. That Beresford be also released provided he promises not to molest Miss Hamilton. And he cancels all damages pronounced against Mrs. Hamilton by the Paris Parlement."

## (3)

In his autobiographical notes Hamilton Rowan makes no direct reference to this family episode. He refers merely to Sarah Dawson's "good-sense and propriety in many different and embarrassing situations." Mrs. Hamilton, having obtained from Louis XVI the cancellation of the decree given against her by the Parlement of Paris, decided that it would be wiser not to return to England until the storm had subsided. She rented from Lord Southwell a little house in the Rue de Mousseau, called the Petit Hôtel de Choiseul, looking over the Choiseul gardens. Sydney for her part was sent to complete her interrupted education at the convent of Petit St. Cyr near Versailles. It was not until much later that she was reunited with her elderly husband.

Meanwhile, as I have said, Hamilton Rowan had fallen in love with Sarah Dawson. She was the daughter of Walter Dawson of Lisanisk, Co. Monaghan, and her father had placed her in the care of his former neighbour, Mrs. Hamilton, in order that she might receive an English education. Hamilton Rowan described her in later life as "possessed of great personal beauty and innate elegance of manner." This is a colourless phrase. Her portrait at Killyleagh, dressed in a blue gown, suggests character rather than loveliness. She was certainly strong-minded, persistent, loyal; she stuck to her erratic husband throughout his later misfortunes and battled for him until she wore down the prejudices of the English authorities by sheer persistence. He remained passionately in love with her all his life. "My little Dawson," he calls her before they were married, "my little stranger." He wrote long letters to her when they were engaged and some of them have been preserved. He tells her of every detail in his rooms in Paris, of the marble slab supported upon a gilt frame under the large mirror; of another mirror above the mantelpiece "so well placed that I wish my Dawson were here to look at herself"; of his bedroom hung with blue flock-paper with blue curtains to the bed and blue velvet chairs; of the dirty deal table standing, among all this finery, in the middle. He confesses to her his irradicable extravagance: "My dear friend," he writes, "if you are as liable to expense, and have no more resolution, than your friend Hamilton, then Lord have mercy upon us miserable debtors!" He tells her something about his Paris acquaintance. "I expect to be well," he writes, "with the Duc de Chartres; he is in the Swiss Guards." He confesses to her his dislike of music: "of the sing-song of the opera house." "You must know," he writes, "that I don't like singing. I like to hear singing when it proceeds from absolute gaiety unrestrained; but to sing 'Oh how pleasing 'tis to please' with a frown and a wish to be elsewhere I do not love."

The depth of his affection for her is better judged from the heart-broken, self-reproachful, letters which he wrote to her later from his exile in America. "I have," he wrote from Wilmington, "taken a small sheet to compress my sins and confessions; and upon looking over this letter I find that I have said nothing of your beauty. Now my dear deceased friend Mary Wollstonecraft (did you see her when in London?) says *that* ought never to be omitted. Well then,—you are beautiful as good and good as beautiful."

They were married in Paris in 1781 at the Dutch Legation which contained a Protestant chapel. For some time they

lived with Mrs. Hamilton at the Petit Hôtel de Choiseul
where their eldest son, William Gawen, was born. According to the family tradition he should have been christened
Gawen. But it was necessary under French law that a child
should be christened by a priest of his own parish, and Hamilton Rowan was obliged to apply to the curate of the Church
of St. Philippe de Roule. The curate had never heard of the
name Gawen, which did not figure in any saints calendar, and
the easy-going Hamilton Rowan bethought him suddenly of
his old grandfather, Mr. Rowan of Rathbone Place. "Let
him be called William also," he said, and William Gawen the
boy was called.

From the Petit Hôtel de Choiseul they moved to a house
of their own at Epinay near St. Denis. They appear to have
spent most of their time with the Irish immigrants in the
French service—with Chevalier Whyte, colonel of the Irish
Foot, with the Chevalier O'Gorman, with Count Wall. Yet
they also moved in higher circles. They accompanied the British Ambassadress, the Duchess of Manchester, when she was
presented to Marie Antoinette—"then," comments Hamilton
Rowan, "in high glory." They frequented the Orléans
circle. They dined with the Foreign Minister, Vergennes,
at Versailles. But neither Rowan himself, nor Sarah seem
to have been in the least interested in these associations.
He makes no comment at all upon the last years of the *ancien
régime*.

From time to time, during that first year of marriage, they
would drive out to St. Cyr and visit Sydney in her convent.
They were received in the common parlour and had to sign
their names in a book. On one of such visits Hamilton Rowan
was surprised to find that when he had given his name, the
main gates of the convent were flung wide open and that he
was conducted straight to the private parlour of the Lady
Abbess, by whom they were both invited to dinner. "I understand," said the Abbess in the course of dessert, "that in England ecclesiastics are permitted to marry." Hamilton Rowan

assured her that this was in fact the case. To his increasing embarrassment he derived from the subsequent course of conversation the impression that the Lady Abbess believed him to be, not an ecclesiastic merely, but also an Archbishop. In seeking to disillusion her on that point he found that she had been misled by reading his signature in the book. He had signed himself "Arch. Hamilton Rowan."

(4)

In reading the memoirs of those who took part in great political movements or who witnessed tragic events, one is often irritated by their lack of any sense of actuality. I am annoyed with my great-great-grandfather for recounting such trivial details and for omitting from his records the many illuminating symptoms and incidents which he must have witnessed. He arrived in Paris at the time when Turgot's reforms had been abandoned and he lived there throughout Necker's fantastic experiments. It was not that he was uninterested in politics; in fact his violent misunderstanding of politics proved his ruin. It was not that he shared with his generation and class that reticence which was supposed to be a sign of good-breeding; his indiscretion at moments flamed like lighted hay. Yet the memoirs which he compiled for the enlightenment of his descendants only serve to increase their bewilderment. He dines with Vergennes, and yet he tells us nothing of the glories of Versailles or of the last stages of the American War; he tells us merely a foolish story about the style of his coachman's wig. He is "well with the Duc de Chartres," but he makes no mention of the Palais Royal circle or of the opposition which even then was forming around the future Philippe Egalité. Did he meet that horrible woman, Madame de Genlis, and see the lovely Pamela playing as an infant at her knee? Did he accompany the Duc to masonic meetings and share those philosophic questionings which sapped the certitude of the French governing class? Was he, again I ask myself, a stupid as well as an unobservant man? It is infuriating that the ideas and illusions which during those important years gave such a twist to his character should cast no single shadow upon the uniform emptiness of his autobiography. Yet he must have been something more in those days than a happy married man rowing idly with his wife and babies on the Seine.

It is only fair to Hamilton Rowan to remember that the original text of his autobiography is not available. He bequeathed it on his death to his friend Thomas Kennedy Lowry with the request that it might be prepared for publication. Mr. Lowry, however, was too busy to execute this task and transferred it to the incompetent hands of Dr. Hamilton Drummond. It was under his editorship that the Autobiography was published in Dublin in 1840. The original text, which may or may not have thrown a sharper light upon its author's character, has disappeared. I suspect that it was destroyed by my great-aunt Fanny or my great-aunt Jane. The printed volume and a few letters are all that remain.

Dr. Drummond appears himself to be aware that the memoirs lack inner transparency. "The autobiography," he confesses in his introduction, "is written with great plainness and simplicity, its object being merely to serve as a record of facts. Accordingly its author never writes for effect, nor indulges in sentimentality or description. On the contrary, he has studiously suppressed the warmest emotions of his heart, as if he felt ashamed, or thought it beneath the dignity of his character to give them expression. He could write well and express himself strongly; but he did not court the graces of style, and it was altogether repugnant to his taste to give a meretricious colouring to any transaction in which he was engaged."

He was not an uninteresting man; people as different as Curran and Clare, as Tone and Castlereagh, regarded him with sympathetic perplexity. His personality impressed itself sharply upon his contemporaries. He had quite a virile mind. Yet his tall figure stalks through his own autobiography without paying much attention either to himself or to his surroundings and there are moments when one wonders whether he was aware of the fantastic pattern which his actions wove. I understand him best when I see him mirrored in the personality of his great-grandson, my own uncle, Gawen Rowan Hamilton. They each wandered through life, aloof and feckless, touching the surface of many things, but too lazy and too bored to penetrate underneath. Possessing sufficient curiosity of mind to welcome new ideas, he had not the mental muscle to form those ideas into shapes adapted to his own capacity. Inquisitive and impulsive, he allowed himself to be caught in currents of feeling, the force and consequence of which he was too lazy, or too optimistic, to examine. Conscious that he possessed a certain originality of temperament, a certain rapidity of intuition, he mistook these surface movements for superior intelligence, and was irked by the fact that his own friends and family were not as impressed by his powers as he was himself. Indolent and impatient he took short cuts with his own passage through life, finding it easier and quicker to win the admiration of the many than by slow effort to establish his reputation with the few. His desire to be exceptional induced him to become eccentric; and in the end his noblest qualities—his loyalty, his hatred of the oppressor and his love for the oppressed—were themselves twisted by vanity into unreasonable shapes. Realizing that his career was verging upon the farcical he transformed it deliberately into a tragedy; he turned his vanity into pride, his loyalties into conspiracy, his convictions into obstinacy, his love into hate. Refusing to admit that he had been wrong, he exaggerated his mistakes until they became a destiny. Too proud to step backwards, he strode forwards with unmeasured strides.

I can understand that a man who had made so foolish a failure of his life should hope by explaining nothing to avoid the necessity of explaining himself away. Viewed from that angle, the very reticence of his autobiography is revealing. It suggests a secret which was never there.

In 1784 Hamilton Rowan and his young wife decided to leave France. They thought at one time of settling in England and of buying a property in Lincolnshire, a county with which Hamilton Rowan was familiar. Sarah, however, hankered after the country of her birth. They crossed to Ireland and rented a small house near Naas in Co. Kildare.

# IV

## THE VOLUNTEERS, 1778-1786

Danger of discussing Irish politics or history—Differences between
the English and the Irish attitude towards law and property—
Inconsistency of English policy towards Ireland—The problem of
security—The disabilities of the Catholics and the Dissenters—
Unfair commercial legislation—Origins of the Patriot Movement
—The Irish Revolution of 1782—Grattan's Parliament—Its fun-
damentally false position—The Killyleagh Volunteers—The Volunteers become political—The Convention of 1783 a fiasco—William Drennan—Hamilton Rowan espouses the cause of emancipation and reform–The address of the Killyleagh volunteers.

### (1)

THIS book is a study of the interaction of sentiment and reality;
it is not a study of Irish politics or history.

I was told a story recently about a major in the West Kent
Yeomanry, upon whom, while he was strolling in a garden
at Sidcup, there settled a queen bee. The major did not at
once observe the queen, and in a few seconds the whole swarm
followed, clustering and quivering with that blind sense of
function which gives to bees and nazis so acute and relent-
less an intensity of purpose. The major was a brave man;
he had fought at Zillebecke and on Gallipoli; he remained
stationary while his panic-stricken family telephoned for an
apiarist; the swarm was hived and the major lived thereafter
to tell the story of his amazing presence of mind. Yet for
the man who is so inadvertent as to allow the queen bee of
Irish politics to settle even for an instant upon his person,
there is no bee-keeper with gauze around his hat to douse the

swarm with puffs of smoke; however great his presence of mind, however firm his imperturbability, it will profit him but little to stand stock-still hoping that the bees will soar off into the June sky intent upon their nuptial flight. He will be stung and stung and stung again. I shall not therefore allow the bee of Irish politics to settle on this book. For I know that it is useless to affirm that my attitude to each contending party is one of benevolent neutrality; that I wish equally well both to the six and to the twenty-six counties; or that I hope that the day may come when they will forget their present animosities, when the whole thirty-two counties will be peopled by United Irishmen. It is no use at all saying that sort of thing. The Irish do not want anyone to wish them well; they want everyone to wish their enemies ill. No Irishman is happy if you agree with him; he is only happy if you express passionate distaste for those with whom he is at variance. And since I regard each side as equally justified, equally pig-headed, equally dull, I am aware that any political opinions which I might indicate or assert would have no success at all.

Yet if Hamilton Rowan's strange behaviour from 1784 onward is to be conveyed with any clarity it is essential to give some slight description, not only of Irish conditions at the time, but of the circumstances which preceded those conditions.

The Irish themselves have no sense of the past; for them the present began on October 17, 1171, when Henry II landed at Waterford. For them history is always contemporaneous and current events are always history; nor can they observe the Killyleagh volunteers drilling either in 1785 or 1913 without their minds dwelling passionately either upon the glorious or disgraceful battle of the Boyne. I have no such hereditary emotions. I shall tell the main facts as calmly and as objectively as I can.

The eternal divergence between the English and the Irish conception of life and politics was due, not only to differences

of race, language and religion, but also to the fact that the
Irish remained immune to the three great formative influences
by which the English way of life was moulded. They were
untouched by the Roman occupation, almost untouched by
the Norman occupation, and wholly untouched by the Reformation; neither Roman Law nor the feudal system came to
mould their attitude towards the State; such Norman barons
as settled in Ireland were rapidly assimilated; Ireland experienced no Huss, no Wickliffe and no Luther; and the Irish conception of law and property remained a specifically Irish conception; it was a tribal conception, it was almost communal. It
took the English some eight hundred years to ascertain this
fact.

Until the 24th May, 1486, the English Government paid
but little attention to Ireland. On that day, however, Lam-
bert Simnel, the fair-faced son of an Oxford carpenter, was
crowned as Edward VI in Dublin Cathedral. Similar recog-
nition was given to Perkin Warbeck a few years later. From
then on it became evident both to England and to her enemies
that Ireland was geographically and politically well adapted
as a base for conspiracy or invasion against the safety of the
realm. The theory became established that England's security
depended upon her control of Ireland and to the subsequent
mishandling of that theory the unhappy tangle of Anglo-Irish
relations has been largely due.

The idea of assimilating the Irish was at an early stage
abandoned in favour of ejecting them, of pushing them out-
wards towards the western areas, and of populating the sea-
board of the Irish Channel with immigrants, settlers, undertakers and planters who, it was thought, could be relied upon
to maintain the English interest. The confiscations which
ensued were sometimes undertaken by force, sometimes as
penalties for real or invented rebellions and often by legal
chicanery. Yet whether under Elizabeth or James I, or
Charles I, or Cromwell, or William III the basic purpose was
not so much to reward mendicant courtiers as to create a Prot-

estant Ascendancy in Ireland strong enough to prevent the country being used as a base either of rebellion or invasion against England.

It is easy to present English policy towards Ireland as a succession of purposeless bursts of spoliation, as a series of intermittent gusts of brigandage, succeeded by spells of remorse. The central policy remained none the less a policy of security; the variations of purpose, which distressed Edmund Spenser as they distressed Sir Horace Plunket, were due, not to any uncertainty as to the central policy, but to constant changes of opinion regarding the means by which this purpose could best be carried out. By seeking, at one moment to extirpate the Irish and at the next moment to please them, the English through all those centuries failed to do either. It is easy to describe British policy towards Ireland as that of the cat towards the mouse; but if so it was a cat with a sense of guilt who would have been much happier if the mouse had lived somewhere very far away.

## (2)

For the purposes of this story it is necessary only to define some of the complex conditions which, by the eighteenth century, this system had produced. On the one hand there was the mass of the Irish population—sundered from the English by race, tradition and language; deeply attached to their Church and the remnants of the old tribal system; dumbly resentful of English law and spoliation; and excluded from the government of their country by all manner of disabilities, under which they were not allowed to vote, to serve in Parliament, to hold office, to enter any profession other than the medical profession, to indulge in trade or commerce, to own land or to possess a horse of the value greater than £5. On the other hand you had the descendants of the English settlers, who had formed themselves into a landed aristocracy, who managed the Irish Parliament and who, although many of them had become very Irish in temperament, were yet vividly aware that they depended upon the English connection, and ultimately upon the English army, for the maintenance of their position and properties against the Irish Catholics. And in the third place you had the settlers in Ulster, who under the Test Act were as dissenters also suffering from disabilities, who were puritan in character and republican by tradition, and whose immense capacity for hatred was divided between dislike of the Catholics and dislike of the English aristocracy and connection. Writing to Lord North in 1774 Lord Harcourt had referred to them as "the Presbyterians of the North who in their hearts are Americans." And in truth many of these Ulster dissenters had already emigrated across the Atlantic where they and their Catholic fellow sufferers formed the nucleus of an anti-English element from which we suffer to this day. The resentment aroused by this curious system under which four-fifths of the population were excluded from any part in the life or politics of their country was further envenomed by the selfish economic policy adopted by successive English Governments. The Irish were forbidden to share in the colonial trade and many Acts had been passed in London, such as the Act of 1699, under which Irish commerce was deliberately ruined for the benefit of English merchants. By the middle of the eighteenth century it was obvious to all observers that so indefensible a system could not possibly continue.

I am aware that the most common of all historical errors is to attribute to one generation the political theories and emotions of their successors and to assume that conditions which would have been intolerable in one century must have been equally intolerable two centuries before. I am not passing any moral judgment upon the Irish system; it grew up gradually from a series of causes, some of which were disreputable causes, and some of which were perfectly reputable. All I am saying is that by the middle of the eighteenth century conditions which had seemed tolerable in 1700 appeared intolerable to the generation of 1760. A change was imminent and it came.

The Patriot Movement of 1760-1782 was not essentially an Irish movement and certainly not a nationalist movement. When the English Government (rendered conciliatory by their reverses in America and well aware that the Irish Volunteer Army was in complete physical control of the situation) surrendered to Grattan and accorded to Ireland a Parliament of her own, they were not in fact according to Ireland anything remotely approaching independence. What Burke called "the Irish Revolution" was only partly Irish and certainly not a revolution. The issue at the time was obscured by the emotional cloud in which the eloquence of Grattan had enveloped it. He would stand there in the Irish House of Commons pouring out his incomparable oratory while making great sawing motions with his arms as if scything some invisible swath. "No power on earth," he thundered, "but the King, Lords and Commons of Ireland is competent to bind Ireland." When in May 1782 the reformed Constitution had been granted, Grattan in his great *esto perpetua* speech proclaimed a new and glorious era. "I am now," he triumphed, "addressing a free people." In fact he was addressing nothing of the sort; he was addressing a packed Assembly, chosen and managed by the Protestant aristocracy determined to maintain the privileges of their caste. He had, it is true, secured the abolition of Poyning's Law and the right of the Dublin Parliament to legislate without the approval of the Privy Council at Whitehall. He had secured the abolition of some of the more indefensible Penal Laws under which the Catholics and the Dissenters were treated as untouchables. Yet Grattan's Parliament in fact represented only 450,000 Protestants out of a population of some four and a half million, of whom 3,150,000 were Catholics and some 900,000 Dissenters. The chief officers of the Executive were still nominated under the Great Seal of England and the distribution of posts and patronage still remained in the hands of the descendants of the former undertakers.

I remember as a boy being shown round the austere and lovely building which had once housed Grattan's Parliament. It was the custom of the Protestant Ascendancy in those days to speak with regretful affection of that institution and to refer to the eighteen years between 1782 and 1800 as the time when all the lights were lit in Dublin and when Ireland basked beatifically in their glow. It may well have been that Grattan, dazzled by his own triumph, imagined that he had in fact secured the independence of his country. "Great Britain," he proclaimed, "gives up *in toto* every claim to authority in Ireland." That was not the view of Flood, Grattan's most unscrupulous rival. It was not the view of the Volunteers as we shall shortly see. It was not the view of Theobald Wolfe Tone, at that date a wild Trinity College student of nineteen. "The Revolution of 1782," he wrote later, "was a Revolution which enabled Irishmen to sell at a much higher price their honour, their integrity, the interests of their country; it was a Revolution which, while at one stroke it doubled the value of every borough monger in the Kingdom, left three fourths of our countrymen slaves as it found them."

It is important for English readers to realize this point, since if it were in fact true that the Constitution of 1782 gave to Ireland all that she could reasonably expect and justified Grattan's paeans, then the subsequent agitation might appear factious and unreasonable. Hamilton Rowan arrived in Ireland two years after Grattan's Revolution. Not for one moment did he imagine that the great principles of the American Revolution or the liberties of Ireland had been vindicated or assured.

(3)

Hamilton Rowan, shortly after his arrival in Ireland, enlisted as a private in the Killyleagh Volunteers, who were at that date commanded by his father. Since it was through his association with the Volunteers that he was drawn into the maelstrom of Irish politics some short account is needed of their origins and composition.

On February 21, 1760, Commodore Thurot had landed some 700 French troops at Kilroot Point east of Carrickfergus and seized the castle in which he was able to maintain himself for four days. On April 13, 1778, after the outbreak of the American War, Paul Jones sailed up the Lough and cast anchor off the harbour of Belfast. The people of Ulster, alarmed by the impunity with which the enemy were able to approach their shores, applied to the Dublin Government for military protection. They were informed that the Government could spare no more than a corporal's guard and that they must see to their own defence. The Volunteer Movement thus arose spontaneously and with the approval of the authorities; within a few months the several corps mustered some 80,000 trained men under the command of Lord Charlemont. Lecky has described them as "the flower of the Protestant yeomanry commanded by the gentry of Ireland." They were more than that; they represented, so long as the American War lasted, almost the only armed force in the country. Having been created to resist foreign invasion they determined to use their power to secure legislative reforms. It was mainly owing to the armed menace of the Volunteers that in May 1782 Grattan was able to obtain his Constitution.

Having won his revolution with the assistance of the Volunteers, Grattan hoped ardently that they would either dissolve or cease to interest themselves in the future proceedings of the Irish Parliament. He had no wish at all to find his new constitution at the mercy of a praetorian guard and he earnestly begged the Volunteers "specifically and majestically to close their great work." Much to the embarrassment of their commander, Lord Charlemont, an important section of the Volunteers refused to abstain from politics. At a convention held at Dungannon in September 1783 a proposal was actually brought forward for some form of Catholic Emancipation. Lord Charlemont described this proposal as "the first appearance of that unaccountable frenzy which afterwards became so dangerously epidemical." It was decided that a Grand National Convention should be held in Dublin on November 10, to coincide with a Reform Bill which Flood was to introduce into the Irish Parliament. The Earl Bishop of Derry was chosen as Chairman of the Convention and made a foolish but triumphal entry into Dublin. The procession which preceded and followed the Earl Bishop was organized by George Robert Fitzgerald, who had by then returned from Brussels but had not yet been hanged at Castlebar. The streets of Dublin were gay with the bright uniforms of the several Volunteer Corps and a *coup d'état* was hourly expected under which the Earl Bishop of Derry would assume the leadership of a United and Independent Ireland. The Government on this occasion were, however, better prepared than they had been a year before. English artillery under Lord Burgoyne had been drafted into the capital in sufficient force to inspire the Dublin Parliament with courage and the less revolutionary elements among the Volunteers with doubt. When Flood with violent vulgarity rose to move his motion Sir Boyle Roche rose to inform the Convention that he had been authorized by Lord Kenmare, the leader of the Irish Catholics, to state that the Catholics themselves were content with the concessions already granted and had no desire for any further reforms. This unauthorized and untrue statement took the wind out of Flood's full sails and his motion was voted down by 157 votes to 77. Flood thereafter went to the House of Commons in full regimentals to ask leave to introduce his bill. The Attorney General informed him that the House could not even consider a bill which was ostentatiously backed by armed force. Flood raged and ranted and went so far as to threaten the House that if their actions were such as to "create dissatisfaction" among the Volunteers, a breach of the peace might result. Fitz-

gibbon, then at the outset of his highly successful career, protested against this appeal to violence. The debate continued
until three in the morning but the House stood firm. In spite
of the dragoons of George Robert Fitzgerald, the Volunteers knew that they could never stand up against the artillery
of Lord Burgoyne. Flood's motion was defeated by a large
majority and he returned foaming with rage to face his Volunteer associates in the Rotunda.

The Volunteer Convention, much disconcerted by this fiasco
in the neighbouring House of Commons, continued their sit-
tings for two further days. Already, however, the great impulse of 1782 had spent its force. The Earl Bishop in the
chair bowed and smiled amicably at the patriotic speeches which
succeeded each other with infinite oratory. "The Catholic
question," comments Lecky, "speedily divided the members."
"They were chased," commented Wolfe Tone more bitterly,
"with disgrace and derision from the capital." The more
sober among them had in fact drifted home to their estates
and farms. The less sober continued to regard themselves
as "the armed property of the Nation," and became progres-
sively more and more extreme. Lord Charlemont was deeply
distressed by their uncompromising attitude. "The anxiety,"
he wrote to Dr. Halliday, "which their conduct has occasioned
me is beyond expression and neither my health or spirits can
any longer bear it."

The health and spirits of Lord Charlemont would have been
still further depressed had he known the association which
these recalcitrant Volunteers were already forming or foreseen
the lengths to which even then they were prepared to go.
Lord Charlemont retained the nominal command of the
Volunteers hoping by his influence to mitigate their more
extreme propensities. But the Earl Bishop of Derry was
observed shortly afterwards to leave for the South of France
arrayed in a lilac suit with a volunteer hat cocked upon his
head.

The Great Volunteer Convention of 1783 had failed.

(4)

In Newry at this time there lived a handsome and sensitive young doctor of the name of William Drennan. The son of a Presbyterian Minister of Belfast, Drennan had studied brilliantly at Edinburgh where he had come under the influence of Dugald Stewart. On taking his medical degree he established himself in practice and employed his many idle moments in writing subversive letters to the Belfast newspapers under the pseudonym of "Orrelana; the Irish Helot." In 1789 he transferred himself from Newry to Dublin where, as will be seen, he took an active part in the proceedings of the Society of United Irishmen. Drennan was the gentle type of revolutionary, a man of taste and manners, and one who is remembered in Irish letters as the author of the lyric "When Erin first rose" and the inventor of the phrase "The Emerald Isle." It was Drennan who first instructed Hamilton Rowan in the intricacies of Irish politics and the philosophic republicanism of the Edinburgh school. It was Drennan who first made him aware of the anti-English tendencies then fomenting slowly among the Ulster Dissenters, and above all it is from Drennan's copious letters to his sister and brother-in-law, Mr. and Mrs. Samuel McTier of Belfast, that we get the clearest picture of the gradations by which reform drifted into sedition, and by which the conception of a representative Dublin Parliament under the Crown and Constitution was gradually replaced by the idea of republicanism and separation from England.

Hamilton Rowan, as we have seen, only arrived in Ireland the year after the fiasco of the Rotunda Convention of 1783. He established himself at Rathcoffey with his wife and son. He paid frequent visits to Dublin and spent much of his time at Killyleagh, where he enlisted in the corps of Volunteers commanded by his father. It was customary for the Volunteers on the occasion of their annual inspection by Lord Charlemont to present their commander with an address of welcome in which suitable compliments were much mingled with unsuitable expressions of political opinion. It fell to Hamilton Rowan, a year after his enlistment, to prepare the address to be given to Lord Charlemont by the Volunteer Corps of Killyleagh and Killinchy. The draft of this particular address has not been preserved, but its tone can well be deduced from subsequent manifestoes and from the cold manner in which it was received by Lord Charlemont. "Hamilton Rowan," writes Drennan from Newry in the summer of 1785, "told me that Lord Charlemont had quashed an address he had prepared at Killyleagh. 'Robert Stewart,' says Rowan, 'coincided with his tremulous Lordship and smothered my address.' Rowan is a clever fellow and just looks the thing for a constitutional conspirator. Lord C. is discarding the political Volunteers—that is now an instrument worn to the handle." "If I could think of politics," writes Drennan the next week, "it should be to persuade the people to a separation from England."

Hamilton Rowan for his part was determined to ignore the advice of Lord Charlemont and Robert Stewart and to stimulate his own corps of Volunteers to increased political activity. In 1785 he attended a Volunteer Convention in Dublin as delegate for Co. Down. In May of 1786 he was elected, in succession to his father, as commander of the Killyleagh and Killinchy corps. In accepting this honour he wrote two letters which indicate the trend of his opinions. These letters are worth quoting. The first is addressed to Mr. William McConnell, Secretary of the Killyleagh Volunteers, and runs as follows:

"I think it my duty to lay my general ideas before the community into which I am called. I must own that the torpid state of the volunteers of Ireland distresses me. At the first institution of the volunteer associations, the peace of this nation was endangered by foreign invaders, and the universal obligation of bearing arms for the public defence seemed to be equalled by the zeal with which the people armed themselves; an uniformity of opinion concerning the internal politics of this nation has been concluded; some corps have laid down their arms whilst others have started up; some new links, then, are now necessary; the reformation of the present state of the representation of the people is, in my opinion, the point to which, and to which alone, the volunteers should tend. The constitution is as much endangered now from the corruption and the unconstitutional influence of a few domestic, as it formerly was by a host of foreign, enemies.

"Are the volunteers to be content to meet annually in silent mock parade? Are they, with the arms of peace in their hands, to permit their constitution, which the blood of our ancestors was shed in establishing against open force, to be mouldered down by the corrupt practices of a few? Or are they to stand forth, the guardians of the rights of mankind, and the determined opposers of every kind of tyranny?

"When I was proposed and admitted into the Killinchy company of volunteers, it was not for the parade of the red coat, nor the merriment of a review day; it was to assist in defeating the insidious policy of corrupt courtiers, who decried the institution because they dreaded its virtue. It is with this view that I now accept the honour you are pleased to confer on me; and by these ideas my future conduct will be regulated, and I trust that the company, who have so affectionately called me among them, will cooperate in the noble cause."

His second letter addressed on the same day to the Killinchy Volunteers was even more expressive:

"Among citizens armed for their constitutional as well as national safety, no superiority is known but that of daring most for the public good.

"Preserve, my dear friends, in the constitutional privilege not only of bearing arms, but being familiar in the use of them, which can only be acquired by exercising in bodies.

"Ministers may be insolent, the great and wealthy may be corrupt; but a free and intrepid yeomanry, with the arms of peace and of defence in their hands, will, I trust, preserve this once famous, but now tottering, constitution."

It is clear from these letters that Hamilton Rowan was convinced at the time that it was the duty of the Volunteers to retrieve their lost political power, to cease to be "torpid" and to become again a "free and intrepid yeomanry with the arms of peace and of defence in their hands." For what purposes this armed power ought, in his judgment to be exercised, is less apparent. On the one hand he claims that the power of the Volunteers should be directed to the defence of the "tottering" constitution, meaning thereby Grattan's constitution of 1782. On the other hand he defines their object as one of electoral reform, meaning thereby the grant of suffrage to the Catholics and the Dissenters. And in the third place, it would seem, the "arms of peace" were to be turned against the Dublin clique, the "great and wealthy," the "insidious policy of corrupt courtiers," in opposition to "tyranny" and in defence of the "rights of mankind."

I cannot resist the impression that when he wrote these letters my great-great-grandfather was either concealing his true intentions or else allowing them to become sadly confused. Had he paused, even for a little while, to think, he would have realized that his pronouncements were lacking either in clarity or candour. In asking his Volunteers to pledge themselves to the defence of Grattan's constitution, he was asking them to pledge themselves to the continuance of the privileges guaranteed by that constitution to the "great and wealthy" of the Protestant Ascendancy. In asking them at the same time to use their power to obtain an extension of the suffrage and the rights of mankind against tyranny, he was asking them to take measures by which Grattan's constitution, and by strict logic his own properties and possessions, would be destroyed.

He did not, I fear, possess a logical mind nor had he even a rudimentary sense of consequences. At the time he knew too little of Irish conditions to observe how ingeniously and precariously the proportions of existing power had been poised, or to realize that the displacement of a single pebble might bring the whole artificial structure to the ground. The incantations of Paris rationalism, the intoxicating phrases of the American Declaration of Independence, had bemused his mind; his loathing of unfairness, his detestation of privileged corruption, were so blinding and intense that in the hurry of his exasperation he never paused to consider what particular form of anarchy would supplant the order which he sought to destroy. At that stage at least his hatred of the oppressor was deeper and more impatient than his love, or his consideration, for the oppressed. He did not possess the intelligence of his young neighbour Robert Stewart, whose more critical judgment merged so naturally into the cool controlled convictions of Lord Castlereagh. He burst into Irish politics in a storm of generous emotion, which was French or American in its quality rather than English or even Irish. And before he understood what had actually happened, the clutch of newly acquired, and on the whole uncongenial, loyalties had affixed its pincers to the metal of his mind.

# V

## MARY NEAL, 1788–1791

The persecution of the Neal family–The bad behaviour of Mrs. Llewellyn and Lord Carhampton–Death of Mrs. Neal in Newgate–Mrs. Llewellyn sentenced and pardoned–Hamilton Rowan's pamphlet–Sir Jonah Barrington's account–Hamilton Rowan gains popularity with the Dublin crowd–The bull-baiting episode–The Northern Whig Club–The "green company" of the Volunteers–Theobald Wolfe Tone–The Society of United Irishmen is founded–Tone's manifesto.

### (1)

THE AMERICAN DECLARATION OF INDEPENDENCE of July 4, 1776, had, as we have seen, formed grooves in Hamilton Rowan's brain. The calculating snobbishness, the tight-lipped conventionality, of his mother had in his boyhood given him a distaste for the English aristocracy—a distaste which his own vanity had in later years transmuted into opposition and finally into hostility. He might well have become an easy-going Whig had not English whiggism been identified in his memory with the cantankerous discipline of his grandfather Mr. Rowan and the harsh tribulations of Rathbone Place. His long idle years upon the continent, the lazy expectancy of one who was heir to a large fortune, had induced a sense of wastage and insufficiency. His was an active rather than a contemplative nature, yet he was too indolent and too egoistic to interpret action in terms of service, and too impatient to translate his restless dissatisfaction with his own life and environment into the patient study of reform. Possessing as he did a contradictory rather than an original mind, he sought to satisfy his craving for distinction by exaggerating the differ-

76

ences between himself and his environment, by preferring the unexpected to the wise. Being averse from deep political thought, having no sense either of logic or of consequences, he fell an easy victim to the phraseology of the American Revolution which provided his restless brain with a facile and inspiring short-cut to political philosophy. His thoughts slipped naturally into these emotional formulas, and he came ardently to believe in such "self-evident truths" as the Laws of Nature, the equality of man and the inalienable rights of life, liberty and the pursuit of happiness. It became a growing habit with him to regard all administration, however slipshod or benevolent it might be, as a "long train of abuses and usurpation." The word "tyranny" formed all too readily upon his lips.

On first arriving in Ireland this facile intemperate philosophy took the form of sporadic opposition to all authority, enlivened by a more specific animosity towards his own caste of Anglo-Irish landlords, towards the Protestant Ascendancy as embodied and embattled in the Dublin Castle clique. In 1788, however, an incident occurred which gave a further and perhaps decisive impetus to the Ishmael within him; he discovered as a result of this incident that, sweet though it might be to gird at tyrants, it was even sweeter to stand out as the protector of the oppressed. For the first time he tasted the strong wine of mob applause.

In Dublin at that date there lived a barber of the name of John Neal. He was a disreputable man, much given to drunkenness, and he lived with his second wife and the children of his first marriage in a squalid quarter of the town. In the next street was a house of ill fame kept by a Mrs. Llewellyn and her friend or "bully," a man of the name of Edgeworth. On the night of April 14 Mary Neal, the barber's daughter, then aged twelve years, was enticed into the house of Mrs. Llewellyn where she was violated by Lord Carhampton.

The story came to the ears of Hamilton Rowan who at once persuaded the barber and his wife to bring an action for abduc-

tion against Mrs. Llewellyn.   The latter was foster-sister to
Lord Carhampton and influence was at once applied to prevent the case being heard.   It was first stated that Mary Neal
was well known in the district as a child-prostitute and that she
had often, with her father's consent and encouragement, visited Mrs. Llewellyn's home in a professional capacity.   Evidence was obtained from one Mary Duffy, an acknowledged
prostitute who lived in the Neals' tenement, that she had on
more than one occasion accompanied Mary Neal to Mrs.
Llewellyn's house.   Hamilton Rowan countered this move
by canvassing from house to house in the district and obtaining certificates of Mary's character from the neighbours.   The
matter was rapidly becoming a public scandal and Lord Carhampton and Mrs. Llewellyn were alarmed.   The bully
Edgeworth induced a second prostitute of the name of Anne
Molyneux to bring a charge of theft against the whole Neal
family.   Mary was charged with having robbed Anne Molyneux of the sum of 18s.   Anne Neal, the step-mother, was
charged with having robbed her of 9s. 9d.   John Neal was
charged with having robbed her of a bottle of wine.   The
charge against Mary was dismissed.   But the magistrates ordered that she should be removed from her home and lodged
in the poor-house, or "House of Industry," under the charge
of the apothecary, Mr. Hunt.   John and Anne Neal were
committed to Newgate.   On the first night of her imprisonment Anne Neal had a miscarriage and died.   The scandal
grew in volume.

Hamilton Rowan at once brought a charge against Edgeworth for subordination to perjury.   Anne Molyneux turned
King's evidence, admitting that she had never even known the
Neal family and that she had been paid by Edgeworth to bring
the charge.   It also transpired that Edgeworth had for years
lived on the proceeds of Mrs. Llewellyn's trade, that he had
bribed the policeman to arrest the Neals, and that he had done
all this in order to prevent the Neal family from bringing
their action against Mrs. Llewellyn.   He was found guilty and

sentenced to be placed in the pillory and to serve twelve months in prison.

On being released from Newgate John Neal, for the second time a widower, persisted, at Hamilton Rowan's instigation, in prosecuting Mrs. Llewellyn for abduction. She was found guilty and sentenced to be hanged. Pressure was applied to the Lord Lieutenant who granted Mrs. Llewellyn a free pardon on the ground that Mary Neal had for long been known as a professional street-walker.

Hamilton Rowan was enraged. He published a pamphlet entitled "A brief investigation of the sufferings of John, Anne and Mary Neal." In this pamphlet he told the whole story from the beginning as an instance of the "interference of power and wealth in opposition to misery and innocence." He went further. He induced Mrs. Hamilton Rowan to drive down to the House of Industry, to remove Mary Neal from the care of Mr. Hunt, and to bring her back in triumph to Rathcoffey. So soon as Mary had recovered from her ordeals he took her up to Dublin to present a petition to the Lord Lieutenant. He made it clear that his action was based, not upon any desire to have Mrs. Llewellyn hanged, but upon the injustice of basing her pardon upon the guilt of Mary Neal. The latter, in her petition to His Excellency, protested against "being soiled with a guilt her soul abhors and her body never voluntarily submitted to." The petition was rejected. Mrs. Llewellyn was released, abandoned her business in Dublin, and retired to a cottage on Lord Carhampton's estate at Luttrelstown. Mary Neal remained for a while a member of Hamilton Rowan's household. "Her subsequent character and conduct," records Dr. Hamilton Drummond, "were not such as to requite the care of her benefactor or justify the interest she had excited in the public mind." Hamilton Rowan for his part, found himself regarded thereafter as the champion of the virtuous poor against the wicked rich. He enjoyed the popularity which this function gave him.

(2)

In his *Personal Sketches of his own Times* Sir Jonah Barrington has left us a vivid impression of the effect made upon Hamilton Rowan by the sad episode of Mary Neal.

"As a philanthropist," he writes, "he certainly carried his ideas even beyond reason, and to a degree of excess which I really think laid in his mind the foundation of all his enthusiastic proceedings, both in common life and in politics. . . . In 1708 the humour of Hamilton Rowan, which had a sort of Quixote tendency to resist all oppression and to redress every species of wrong, led him to take up the case of Mary Neil [*sic*] with a zeal and enthusiastic perseverance which nobody but the Knight of La Mancha could have exceeded. Day and night the ill-treatment of this girl was the subject of his thoughts, his actions, his dreams; he went about preaching a kind of crusade in her favour. Yet there were not wanting persons who doubted her truth, decried her former character, and represented her story as that of an imposter. This not only hurt the feeling and philanthropy, but the pride, of Hamilton Rowan; and he vowed personal vengeance against all her calumniators, high and low."

It would seem that the hilarity aroused in some circles by the Mary Neal episode was particularly rampant among the young barristers of the town. Many of them had averred that they knew from personal experience that Mary Neal was, to say the least, highly precocious for her age. These sallies reached the ears of Hamilton Rowan who determined to silence them for ever. The barristers at that date used to meet regularly at a dining club of which Sir Jonah Barrington was a member. Their meeting one evening was interrupted by the incursion of Hamilton Rowan. Barrington has told the story so vividly that I produce it in his own words:

"One day, whilst dining with our usual hilarity, the servant informed us that a gentleman below stairs desired to be admitted for a moment. We considered it to be some brother barrister who requested permission to join our party, and desired him to be shown up.

"What was our surprise, however, on perceiving the figure that presented itself—a man who might have served as a model for Hercules, his gigantic limbs conveying an impression of almost supernatural strength; his shoulders, arms and broad chest were the very emblems of muscular energy; and his flat, rough countenance, overshadowed by enormous dark eyebrows, and deeply furrowed by strong lines of vigour and fortitude, completed one of the finest, yet most formidable, figures I had ever beheld.

"He was well dressed; close by his side stalked in a shaggy Newfoundland dog of corresponding magnitude, with hair a foot long, and who, if he should be voraciously inclined, seemed well able to devour a barrister or two without overcharging his stomach. . . . His master held in his hand a large yellow-knotted club, slung by a leathern thong round his great wrist; he had also a long small-sword by his side.

"This apparition walked deliberately up to the table; and having made his obeisance with seeming courtesy, a short pause ensued, during which he looked round upon the company with an aspect, if not stern, yet ill-calculated to set our minds at ease either as to his or his dog's ulterior intentions.

" 'Gentlemen,' at length he said, in a tone and with an air at once so mild and courteous, nay so polished, as fairly to give the lie, as it were, to his gigantic and threatening figure, 'Gentlemen! I have heard with great regret that some members of this club have been so indiscreet as to calumniate the character of Mary Neil which, from the part I have taken, I feel identified with my own. If any present have done so, I doubt he will have the candour and courage to avow it. Who avows it?'

"The dog looked up at him again; he returned the glance, but contented himself for the present with patting the animal's head and was silent. So were we.

"He repeated the demand, elevating his tone each time, thrice: 'Does any gentleman avow it?'

"A faint buzz now circulated round the room, but there was no answer whatsoever. Communication was cut off and there was a dead silence. At length our visitor said with a loud voice, that he must suppose that if any gentleman had made any observations or assertions against Mary Neil's character he would have had the courage and spirit to avow it. 'Therefore,' he concluded, 'I shall take it for granted that my information was erroneous; and, in that point of view, I regret having *alarmed* your society.'

"And without another word he bowed three times very low, and retired backwards towards the door, his dog also backing out with equal politeness, where with a salaam doubly ceremonious, Mr. Hamilton Rowan ended his extraordinary interview."

(3)

Hamilton Rowan's espousal of the cause of Mary Neal gained him a high reputation among the proletariat of Dublin. Here was an aristocrat and a Protestant who put justice above privilege or caste; a man who was prepared to devote his money and his time to the defence of the oppressed; a man who dared publicly to expose the corruption of the governing clique; a man who had accompanied a wretched slattern of the back alleys into the presence of the Lord Lieutenant himself. He much enjoyed the popularity which he had thus acquired; he welcomed the untidy visitors who would appear at Rathcoffey in the hope of enlisting his sympathy and his purse in the cause of some new grievance; he was delighted when, on his increasingly frequent visits to Dublin, the populace would recognize his brown and yellow liveries and cheer his carriage as it rattled by.

It is not surprising therefore that before long he found himself again in his new role of a Tribune of the people, involved in a conflict with authority. On St. Stephen's day, Decem-

ARCHIBALD HAMILTON ROWAN
(*From a Bust at Killyleagh*)

See page 82

HAMILTON ROWAN IN EDINBURGH

*See page 108*

ber 27, 1789, a crowd of hooligans was observed driving a young bull towards a field on the outskirts of the city. They were accompanied by many dogs and they drove the bull along with sticks and shouts and stones. Some sensitive citizen of Dublin, observing this procession, deduced rightly that the crowd intended to indulge in the cruel sport of bull-baiting. The matter was at once reported to Sheriff Vance who arrived at the field accompanied by a guard of soldiers. The crowd, enraged at the interruption of their sport, pelted the sheriff and his guard with oyster shells. Vance ordered the military to open fire and four persons in the crowd were killed.

Great indignation was aroused by this incident and the families of the victims were encouraged to prosecute the Sheriff for murder. They applied to Hamilton Rowan for assistance, asking him to attend a meeting in St. Mary's parish to raise funds for the prosecution. He at first demurred on the ground that his attendance might "be construed into a vain attempt at popularity, particularly as his name had been obtruded perhaps too often on the public." On reaching Dublin, however, and enquiring into the circumstances, he convinced himself that Vance's action had in fact been "a diabolical exercise of power." He therefore threw himself into the case with his accustomed impulsive energy and agreed to guarantee the cost. The case was heard in the Court of King's Bench and Vance was acquitted.

Hamilton Rowan, who had been obliged to pay legal expenses to the amount of £90, consoled himself by writing an introduction to the published report of the proceedings. His usual style was hampered by a desire not to be committed for contempt of court, but even so it must be confessed that his introduction is not a very trenchant document. On the one hand he defends the manly pastime of bull-baiting on the ground that "at Cambridge there were constant bull-baitings under the very eye of the Vice-Chancellor and all the doctors of law and divinity." On the other hand he contended that

Vance had not shown due circumspection when he ordered his men to fire. "The soldiers," he writes, "when St. Paul was shipwrecked on Melita would have put him to death lest he escape, but the centurion, more humane, saw not the necessity."

Such episodes although they increased his popularity with the lower orders, do not seem at that stage to have earned him the enmity of the great Protestant families. His charming courtesy, the extreme elegance of his dress and manners, seem for long to have persuaded them that Hamilton Rowan was no more dangerous than any other harmless eccentric who had lived too long upon the continent and who would soon settle down to enjoy his large fortune and the excellent anomalies of the Anglo-Irish system.

He was regarded at the time as a typical Whig and as such was welcomed as a member of the Northern Whig Club at Belfast, which was controlled by such respectable liberals as Lord Charlemont, Lord Moira, Lord de Clifford, and Robert Stewart, shortly to become Lord Castlereagh. The resolutions passed and published by this Club were more violent in appearance than in reality. In April 1790, at a meeting at which Gawen Hamilton took the chair and Robert Stewart was present, a resolution was passed to the effect that "when an unmasked and shameless system of ministerial corruption manifests an intention to sap the spirit, virtue and independence of Parliament, it is time for the people to look to themselves." At the banquet which followed, the toasts were "The glorious and immortal memory," "The Rights of the People," "May the example of one Revolution prevent the necessity of another," "A speedy and happy establishment of Gallic Liberty" and "Our Sovereign Lord the People."

Two years later, on November 5, 1792, at a meeting held under Hamilton Rowan's own chairmanship, the Northern Whig Club congratulated the revolutionary armies of France upon their victories at Valmy and Jemappes. It also congratulated Ulster upon "the rapid decay of bigotry and prejudice." But the Northern Whig Club were not in favour of any emancipation of the Catholics and still less in favour of any loosening of the English interest. A proposal brought forward by Hamilton Rowan which advocated "liberty to all sects and denominations of Irishmen" was not passed unanimously. It was evident that the Northern Whig Club of Belfast were not anxious to push their democratic principles too far.

The club was ridiculed by Lord Clare in Dublin as little more than an association "for eating and drinking." When war was declared by France against Great Britain in 1793 it died of inanition. Its members became divided and dispersed. Already in May 1791 William Drennan had foreseen that the Whigs of Belfast were doomed by the fact that their avowed principles clashed horribly with their private interests. Writing to Samuel McTier he expressed his contempt for the association of the Northern Whigs. What was required was something far more secret and seditious. "A society," he wrote, "having much of the secrecy and some of the ceremonial of Freemasonry; so much secrecy as might communicate curiosity, uncertainty and expectation. Such a Society should aim, not merely at emancipation and reform, but at independence and republicanism and should establish connections with France and America."

With these words William Drennan forecast the impending formation of the Society of United Irishmen.

(4)

Among the Belfast volunteers was a company, calling itself "The Green Company" which was mainly composed of small Presbyterian shopkeepers of Scottish origin. This company had formed from among its members a political club directed by a secret committee of eleven, including the young draper Samuel Neilson and Drennan's brother-in-law, McTier. Hav-

ing discovered that the atmosphere of Dublin was not at the
moment propitious for the formation of his revolutionary
brotherhood, Drennan decided to sow the first seeds of his
conspiracy in Belfast. He therefore visited the McTiers in
time for the Bastille celebrations of July 14, 1791.

Stationed in Belfast at that date was an officer of the 64th
Regiment of Foot of the name of Thomas Russell. He was
sympathetic to the views of the Green Company and was admitted into the confidence of the secret committee. He advised them that the first thing they should do was to prepare
a manifesto setting out their ideas and purposes. He added
that he had a friend in Dublin, a brilliant young lawyer of
the name of Theobald Wolfe Tone, who was the very man
required. William Drennan, who had himself aspired to become the intellectual leader and the pamphleteer of the movement, was none too pleased by the introduction of Tone. But
the Committee were shown, and were much impressed by,
Tone's recent pamphlet entitled *An Argument on behalf of
the Catholics of Ireland*. Russell was authorized to get into
touch with Tone and did so immediately. It was in this manner that these cautious Ulster republicans, who were to form
the nucleus of the Society of the United Irishmen, became entangled from the outset with the dynamic, volatile and heroic
personality of Theobald Wolfe Tone.

This sallow and enthusiastic man, with his long lank hair
and enormous nose, was at that date twenty-eight years of age.
He was the son of a bankrupt coachmaker, having been born
in Stafford Street, Dublin, on June 20, 1763. The early bril-
liance which he displayed, the actual vivacity of his conversa-
tional gifts, had earned him a place in the "latin" school and
a pensioner's post at Trinity College. At the age of twenty-
two he eloped with the sixteen-year-old granddaughter of a
clergyman and thereafter studied law in London where he had
chambers at No. 4 Hare Court, Temple. From the first he
manifested a violent distaste for all legal studies. At one moment he tried to enlist in the service of the East India Com-

pany and at the next he devised a scheme for establishing a
military colony in the South Sea Islands. He carried this
scheme to No. 10 Downing Street determined to convince Mr.
Pitt by personal persuasion of the excellence of his proposal.
The Prime Minister was unable to receive him and he vowed
that one day he would force Mr. Pitt to rue this act of dis-
courtesy. He returned to Dublin and was admitted to the
Irish bar. His dislike of the slow precisions of legal practice
was intensified by his early experience on the Leinster circuit.
He possessed all the elements which go to the formation of
a revolutionary character—laziness, penury, domestic worries,
vivacity, fluency, courage and a most impatient mind. His
mortification at his lack of immediate success turned into hatred of the existing order. Tone, there can be no question,
had in him a streak of genius, a strong strain of heroism. The
men whom he inspired and compromised seem small and fum-
bling in comparison.

It was on October 11, 1791, that Tone joined Russell in
Belfast. He was delighted with the strong Jacobin spirit which
prevailed. "Paine's book," he noted in his diary, "is the
Khoran of Belfescu." He had a strange and irritating habit
of calling places and people by classical or Eastern European
nick-names.

Three days later, at 4.0 p.m. on October 14, 1791, he met
the committee of the Green Company in secret session. The
addition of Tone and Russell brought the original eleven to
the number of thirteen. It was at that meeting that the "Society of United Irishmen" was formed. A second and larger
meeting, at which twenty-eight people were present, was held
on October 18. Tone submitted his manifesto to them and
then returned to Dublin. A few weeks later he created the
Dublin branch of the Society, at a meeting held at the Eagle
tavern in Eustace Street. Among the original members of this
branch were Napper Tandy, William Drennan, Simon Butler
and Hamilton Rowan. It was agreed that the objects of the
group should be to "create a united society of the Irish nation—

to make all Irishmen citizens and all citizens Irishmen." As the badge of the Society they adopted a harp surmounted by a cap of liberty and bearing the device "It is new strung and shall be heard."

(5)

The manifesto which Tone drafted and sent to Russell in advance of the meeting of October 1791 was not in itself so very subversive. It pointed out that "the people are deprived of their natural weight in the scale of Government because they are not duly represented in Parliament." It demanded therefore "a more general extension of the elective franchise." It pointed out that "the weight of English influence in the Government of this Country is so great as to require a cordial union among the people to maintain that balance which is so essential to the preservation of our liberties and the extension of our commerce." It lamented "the mistaken policy which has so long divided the people of Ireland," and it pledged the Society to "co-operate heartily in all measures tending to the abolition of distinction between Irishmen."

The sting of the manifesto was to be found rather in its preamble than in the resolutions which it embodied. This preamble ran as follows:

"We have no National Government. We are ruled by Englishmen and the servants of Englishmen, filled, as to commerce and politics, with the short-sighted and ignorant prejudices of their country; and these men have the whole of the power and patronage of Ireland as means to seduce and subdue the honesty and spirit of her representatives in the legislature."

That such comparatively moderate opinions and desires were not wholly expressive of Tone's purposes is evident from the covering letter in which he sent his draft to Thomas Russell:

"The foregoing," he wrote, "contain my true and sincere opinion of the state of this country, so far as in the present juncture it may be advisable to publish it; they certainly fall short of the truth, but truth itself must sometimes condescend to temporize. My unalterable opinion is that the bane of Irish prosperity is the influence of England. I believe that influence will ever be extended while the connection between the two countries continues. Nevertheless, I know that opinion is for the present too hardy, though a very little time may establish it universally. . . . I have not said one word which looks like a wish for separation, though I give it to you and your friends as my most decided opinion that such an event would be a regeneration for this country."

This letter (as indeed most of the letters which passed between the United Irishmen) fell into the hands of the Government who published it in 1793. Tone immediately repudiated any suggestion of secession; he had not, he explained, meant that there should be any complete severance between England and Ireland; all he had meant was that some new form of connection might prove mutually beneficial. His son also denied the implications of this passage. In the biography of his father which he published at Washington in 1828, he described this subversive passage as "playful and theoretical." Yet in view of Tone's subsequent career it is difficult to resist the impression that he deliberately concealed his real intentions from the Protestants of Belfast.

In this, it must be admitted, he showed greater acumen than most of his fellow members. He knew that the northern Protestants, republicans and dissenters though they might be, were imbued with a deep anti-Catholic prejudice and would hesitate to sever the English connection if that would mean that power were transferred to the Catholic majority. He knew that most of them were temporarily intoxicated by the wine of the American and French revolutions and might hesitate to follow him further once these fumes had cleared. He did not, in fact, take either the Volunteers or the United Irishmen very seriously. "The Club," he wrote, "was scarcely formed before I lost all pretensions to anything like influence in their measures."

He described the United Irishmen at a later date as people who "had been more serviceable to their enemies than to their friends." For Tone, unlike most of the patriots of his time, was a determined realist. He used the United Irishmen so long as they were profitable to him, even as he used the Volunteers, the Catholics and the Whigs. But in his heart he cherished the contempt of the man of action for the formulas, the badges, the secret pass-words and the whole mumbo-jumbo of Drennan and his friends. He saw, as others did not see, the inherent falsity of their position; he understood that their personal privileges, prejudices and interests would in the end conflict with the ardent opinions which they proclaimed; and while accurately estimating their value as a disturbing influence, he knew that an independent Ireland (if that were a desirable thing to achieve—and at that stage he was not at all sure that it would be desirable) could only be obtained with the assistance of a foreign army and through a rising of the Catholic peasantry.

# VI

## SEDITIOUS LIBEL, 1792–1794

The Volunteer Review in Belfast–Hamilton Rowan joins Dublin Branch of United Irishmen–The Napper Tandy incident–Hamilton Rowan intervenes on his behalf–The National Guards–The Convention of 1792–The Green Volunteers prohibited–"Citizens to Arms!"–Hamilton Rowan committed for trial–His provocative attitude–The Simon Butler incident–Hamilton Rowan takes a challenge to the Lord Chancellor–He thinks of leaving Ireland–War between France and England.

### (1)

FOR THE moment, however, Tone was very willing to use both the United Irishmen and the Volunteers for what they might be worth. With this in mind he journeyed up to Belfast, the "Belfescu" of his diary, for the third great celebration, on July 14, 1792, of the taking of the Bastille.

Ulster still remained the centre of the United Irishmen, there being by then four clubs in Belfast and many others scattered through the province. In Catholic Ireland the movement still failed to acquire adherents. There was the original Dublin club which Tone had founded the year before and which now held its meetings in the Taylor's Hall, in Back Lane, off the Corn-market. It is significant to note that this hall was also used at the time for the regular meetings of the Freemasons, with whom the United Irishmen were closely connected. A more casual place of meeting was Byrne's bookshop in Grafton Street, and it was through Byrne and his assistant that secret messages were relayed. But the Catholic Committee, to which Tone had recently become the assistant secretary, were far more cautious than their Presbyterian brethren; they looked upon the United Irishmen with suspicion and almost with distaste; they had no desire at all to put themselves in a false position either with Dublin Castle or with the Cabinet in London. It is to his connection with the Catholic Committee that we should perhaps ascribe the hesitancy which is observable in Tone's actions and attitude during the succeeding months.

Not that, upon this his second visit to Belfast, he was over-cautious. The occasion was to be marked by a grand review of the Volunteers—the last review held in the full panoply of their unity and ardour. The review was preceded by a meeting in the Linen Hall to which Tone submitted a draft address demanding electoral reform. The address contained the phrase "We reprobate and abhor the idea that political inequality should result from religious opinions." Napper Tandy and the Presbyterian members of the Society of United Irishmen begged Tone to omit this passage, which they contended would much incense Protestant feeling and which would certainly be voted down. Tone persisted with his original draft, and such was the force of his personality that it was adopted with enthusiasm. They dined thereafter at the Donegal Arms—Napper Tandy became rapidly insensible; Tone was flushed and excited by the triumph he had won. "God bless everybody!" he noted enthusiastically in his diary. "Broke my glass thumping on the table."

The Review, on that July 14, 1792, was a symbolic affair. The programme of the procession has been preserved and is illustrative of the fictions and fantasies which then swayed men's minds. The president for the day was Major Crawford of Crawfordsburn. The procession was headed by seventeen light dragoons, who were followed by the Flags of the Free Nations bearing topical inscriptions embroidered on the silk. First came the flag of Ireland with the words "Unite and be free." Then the flag of the United States entitled "The Asylum of Liberty." The French flag followed bearing the inscription (since Belfast was a little out of touch with recent political developments in Paris) "The Nation, the Law and the King." There was a flag for Poland, bearing the heartening words "We will support it"; and finally the flag of Great Britain with the words "Wisdom; spirit; and liberality to the people." After the flags came a portrait of Dr. Benjamin Franklin carried high upon an easel. Then followed the first brigade of the volunteers numbering 532 men accompanied by the artillery of the Belfast Blues. Then came what was in fact the key of the whole procession, namely "The Great Standard" borne upon a triumphal car drawn by four horses. This car carried an enormous cartoon, representing on one side "The Releasement of the Prisoners from the Bastille" and on the other side Hibernia in shackles being offered a statue of Liberty by a volunteer. The Great Standard was followed by the second brigade of volunteers, and the procession closed with a portrait of Mirabeau bearing the strange device "Our gallic brother was born in 1789. We are still in embryo."

(2)

Hamilton Rowan, as has been said, joined the Dublin branch of the Society of United Irishmen in the late autumn of 1791. "And thus," he records lightly, "circumstances led me to an acquaintance with the popular leaders in Ireland and transmitted the name of an insignificant individual to posterity."

Drennan was much impressed by Hamilton Rowan and regarded him as a most valuable revolutionary. Tone was not quite so sure. He placed little reliance either in Hamilton Rowan's political judgment or in his willingness, in view of his possessions and family, to go to the uttermost ends of sedition. Tone was not a man to conceal his feelings and the corners of his inquisitive but suspicious mouth were apt to droop in a slight sneer. Hamilton Rowan was determined to prove to this cynical young man that, in the cause of "the people" (he remained throughout his life uncertain what that phrase in fact implied) he was prepared to sacrifice his wealth, his family, his liberty and if need be his life. Tone considered

that he would be more useful at the moment, not as the leader
of an insurrection, not even as a political revolutionary, but as
a man of position, good address, influential connections, and
great personal courage who might serve, in minor ways, as the
armed champion of the United Irishmen in the event of their
cause being publicly traduced.  This conception of his function
involved Hamilton Rowan in a ludicrous intervention on behalf of Napper Tandy.

This ugly, loquacious, drunken and wholly absurd little man
has been immortalized by his inclusion in the four most famous
lines of the "Wearing of the Green":

"I met with Napper Tandy and he took me by the hand,
And he said, 'How's poor old Ireland, and how does she stand?'
'Tis the most distressful country, for it's plainly to be seen
They are hanging men and women for the wearing of the green."

"He acquired celebrity," writes Sir Jonah Barrington, "without being able to account for it," and in truth it is remarkable
that a man of so little real capacity should have started life as
a muddled ironmonger and have ended it as a General in the
army of Napoleon and a national figure in his own country.
He became involved, during his many outbursts and adventures, in many curious episodes, and from each episode he
emerged foolishly, mouthing heroics and grasping a bottle of
brandy in his hand.  The particular episode in which he involved Hamilton Rowan in February of 1792 was neither
more nor less foolish than those which had preceded it and
were to follow.  On February 20 the Solicitor General John
Toler speaking in the Irish House of Commons made a passing
reference to the United Irishmen and a somewhat pointed
reference to Napper Tandy's personal ugliness.  Toler's joke
was not a very good joke in any case, nor was it well expressed.
"I have some papers here," he said, "signed Tobias M'Kena,
with Simon Butler in the chair and Napper Tandy lending his
*countenance*.  It was rather odd they could not contrive to put
a better *face* upon it."  Tandy was much enraged by this reference to his physical disadvantages and was impulsive enough
to ask the Solicitor General for an "explanation."  Toler re-

plied that if he meant by this that he was anxious to fight a duel, he for his part would be glad to await a formal challenge. Tandy was disconcerted by this rejoinder and explained to his friends that his affairs were still in such disorder that he could not risk a personal affray. Toler then started proceedings against him for breach of privilege. Tandy thereupon left Dublin hurriedly and hid himself in the country.

Tone felt that this farcical episode was of a nature to bring the United Irishmen into disrepute. He induced Hamilton Rowan to take the office of Acting Chairman of the Society and to pass a resolution to the effect that the Solicitor General's action was in itself a breach of privilege. Meanwhile Tandy's hiding place had been discovered; he was arrested and brought, amid much general laughter, to the bar of the House. Tone and Hamilton Rowan attended this hilarious scene in their Whig Club uniforms, "which," as Tone remarked, "were rather gaudy." Tandy was committed to Newgate, but since Parliament was prorogued two hours later he was released in circumstances of great merriment. "Poor Tandy," wrote Drennan, "after eighteen years' struggle against his own interest in the public cause, has nearly lost his reputation as a gentleman in a quarter of an hour."

Hamilton Rowan had doubtless hoped that his dramatic appearance on this occasion might provoke a challenge from some member of the House and thus justify his function as the champion of the Society. In spite, however, of his gaudy uniform and truculent manner, the House adjourned for the recess without paying much attention to Napper Tandy or any attention at all to Hamilton Rowan.

It was obvious that if he were to be taken seriously by his former equals or his present fellows some more drastic action would be required. It was not long before an opportunity presented itself.

## (3)

It will be recalled that ever since the fiasco of the Rotunda Convention of 1783 the Volunteers had been split into two wings, the right wing representing the landed gentry and therefore the Protestant ascendancy, the left wing becoming increasingly republican and separatist. Fired by the example and language of the French Revolution this left wing called themselves the "National Guards," adopted a lively green uniform, and sported republican badges. Having boycotted King William's birthday celebrations in 1792 they summoned a Convention to take place in Dublin on December 8. The Government, as would appear from the secret reports now rendered available, realized that this group represented only a small minority of extremists and could be easily suppressed. "I assure you," reported one of their secret informers, "I never saw so small a number of determined-looking men on so large a body. My idea of them is perfectly contemptible. I think with a serjeant's guard I should not be afraid to disarm the whole of them."

It was evident, when the meeting took place on December 8, that this contemptuous report was not without foundation. In the first place those who attended the meeting were conscious that they represented but a tiny residue of those Volunteers who had fought for Grattan's Constitution ten years before. In the second place they were divided even among themselves. Tone, who in September and October had constantly been urging Hamilton Rowan to take a firm stand and to come out into the open, now showed symptoms of hesitation, even of timidity. Napper Tandy was obviously no good at all. Drennan and Hamilton Rowan found themselves abandoned and alone. "Many in the Convention," wrote Drennan on December 8, "regard us as republicans and sinners and don't like to have communication with us. Tomorrow will produce something. It is said that the Riot Acts will be read to the Volunteers if they assemble."

On the following day, December 9, 1792, the Government did in fact take action. They issued a proclamation which, while praising the old or "loyal" volunteers, denounced the Green Volunteers as the enemies of the Constitution and warned them that if they gathered together on parade they would be regarded as "an unlawful assembly."

"In short," wrote Drennan to McTier, "the proclamation is levelled at the First National Battalion, nicknamed National Guards. It did not prevent Hamilton Rowan and one or two other Protestants from walking in the streets with their green uniform and side-arms. The mob surrounded them and huzzaed much. They spoke to them requesting peace and quietness and begging them particularly to have respect and proper behaviour to the soldiery. The Catholics, who first originated the idea of this corps, are now afraid and would rather have prevented any meeting. Tone was warm on that side, but Rowan deemed it his duty to stand forth as one of the Protestant volunteers leaving the Catholics to act as their wisdom and prudence might suggest. The Catholics have damped the new volunteers which they originally moved, and Rowan, Tandy, etc., are left in the lurch. Rowan will be as mad as the rugged Russian bear. Butler swears to me that Tone has been bought off."

A week later, on December 16, 1792, the more determined members of the National Guard held a meeting in the house of Pardon, a fencing master, in Cope Street. It was a long empty room containing a small gallery at one end and a large table in the centre mounted upon trestles. Upon the table was a bundle of papers, including copies of a pamphlet prepared by Drennan and entitled "Citizens to Arms!" In this pamphlet the volunteers were urged to assemble in arms in defiance of the government proclamation and to press for a convention. People walked about talking in groups and there was much hubbub in the room. Lieutenant Skinner, a junior officer of the Volunteers, observing one or two people leaning over the balustrade of the gallery, took some copies of the pamphlet from the table and handed them up to the spectators. Lieutenant Skinner, it would seem, was a tall man bearing some personal resemblance to Hamilton Rowan. Information was at once lodged at Dublin Castle to the effect that it was Hamilton Rowan who had "distributed" the pamphlet.

On the morning of December 21 the Sheriff Carleton called at Dominick Street and "in a very civil manner" arrested Hamilton Rowan for having distributed inflammatory handbills. He appeared before Judge Downes and was immediately granted bail for £200. Under the terms of this bail he was obliged to appear at the Court of King's Bench in person when that court was in session. During the vacation he was allowed his liberty without let or question. Regularly he appeared but no trial was called.

It is important to note that although he was committed for trial in December 1792 his trial did not actually take place until January 1794. Hamilton Rowan himself attributed this delay to the desire of the administration to wait until in October 1793 Jack Giffard had become Sheriff and when they knew they could count upon a packed jury. It is more probable that Dublin Castle did not take Hamilton Rowan too seriously and hoped that he would either break his bail and escape to England or else behave reasonably and permit them to quash the indictment.

He did not behave reasonably. And in the interval between his indictment and his trial several incidents and events occurred which placed him in a position of great danger. He remained unaware of this danger although he received many hints from high quarters. "Hamilton Rowan," whispered the Speaker to a friend who was bound to repeat the warning, "does not know the risk he runs, for we have evidence against him which would touch his life."

He continued to conduct himself with violence and indiscretion.

(4)

The warrant issued against Hamilton Rowan caused panic among the remaining members of the National Guard. "Tandy's volunteers," wrote Drennan, "are to disband next Sunday, but Tandy is too plainly timid. Rowan's will probably disband, though but fifty strong and not a Catholic among them. He is vexed to the soul with them but keeps his brow as smooth as he can." In fact, within a few days, his little band of fifty men melted away and dispersed to their homes. Hamilton Rowan in despair resigned his commission in the volunteers, although as a gesture he retained the uniform of a private. "He is glad," wrote Drennan, "to get out of a set of men who have neither the spirit nor the manners of gentlemen. I wish Lord Charlemont were ousted from the volunteers and Rowan made their General. It is a place suited to him and he to it. . . . Tone, Russell, Emmet, etc., are so entwined with Catholic trammels that they cannot act as their heart leads them. There is, as Mr. Burke says, some difference in blood. The Mountgarret blood is heroic. Tandy, Dowling, etc. are not gentlemen. Rowan *is*, every inch of him, body and soul." Nor was Drennan ever able to conceal his "unaccountable repugnance" for Wolfe Tone.

It cannot be said that Rowan, between his indictment in December 1793 and his trial in January 1794, did anything to conciliate authority. He would still stride about the streets of Dublin in his green uniform, clasping his heavy club and accompanied by a Newfoundland or a Great Dane. He was under the illusion, an illusion shared by many dog-maniacs, that it was possible for human beings to communicate with these animals in their own tongue. He would thus, much to the astonishment of the passers-by, make yapping noises at his dogs, interspersed by short sharp barks. But his real orders were given by a gentle touch of his great hands upon their necks.

Thus accoutred and accompanied he would invade the theatres of Dublin and stand up in his place when the band played "God save the King" clamouring for the "Volunteer March." The people in the stalls would gaze at his vast figure with amusement and surprise. The people in the gallery would cheer his outright patriotism. He would stalk back on foot to Dominick Street with the mob buzzing behind.

Two incidents occurred during this year of anticipation which enabled him once again to affirm his courage and independence. In January of 1793 a secret committee of the Irish House of Lords met to consider the agitations of the past year. Their deliberations led to the Convention Bill which prohibited the meeting of any representative or delegated assembly other than Parliament itself and also to the Militia Act which prepared for the creation of a National Militia as a counterweight to the Undisciplined Volunteers, and as a means of coping with the peasant jacquerie which were causing disturbances under the name of "the Defenders." The United Irishmen were bound by their principles and pledges to oppose these two enactments. They published a "series of observations" in which they contended that the recommendations of the House of Lords Committee constituted a breach of privilege. This paper had been drafted and signed by Simon Butler and Boyd, who were themselves tried for breach of privilege, fined £500, and committed for six months to Newgate, where they entertained their friends royally at the expense of the United Irishmen.

In the course of their trial Fitzgibbon, who was shortly to become Earl of Clare, made some pertinent but insulting remarks regarding the personal conduct of Simon Butler. The latter was brother to Lord Mountgarret, and a member of the Irish Bar. Fitzgibbon had called him a disgrace, not only to his class, but "to His Majesty's gown which you wear." Butler regarded this as an unreasonable affront and, having brooded over the incident in the intervals of his champagne suppers at Newgate, asked Hamilton Rowan to act for him in the matter "as his friend." He begged him to call upon the Lord Chancellor and to demand an apology for this outrageous remark.

Hamilton Rowan asked for an appointment with the Lord Chancellor and was received next day. He informed Lord Fitzgibbon that had the matter been one between two private gentlemen his course would be plain and easy. He confessed, however, that "His Lordship's situation as Lord Chancellor embarrassed him." The Lord Chancellor replied that he had used the expression advisedly and that he would use it again. Hamilton Rowan then withdrew.

It would seem, however, that Lord Fitzgibbon was not un-impressed by the enormous, stately, and exquisitely polished gentleman who had intervened so foolishly on Simon But-ler's behalf. On the following morning the door-bell rang in Dominick Street and a visitor was announced in the person of Colonel Murray, an old friend of the Hamilton family. "A pretty piece of work you have made," blustered the Colonel, "taking a challenge to the Lord Chancellor." Hamilton Rowan was himself conscious that circumstances and Simon Butler had conspired to place him in a false position. He was dispirited at the time, not merely by the desertion of Tone and Russell and the rest, not merely by the cowardice of Napper Tandy but by abundant evidence that there were traitors in the inner circle of the United Irishmen. Their innermost secrets, it would seem, were reported to Dublin Castle within a few hours. Who were the informers? Was it Russell, or Tone or even Drennan himself? His confidence in his fellow conspirators was badly shaken.

Colonel Murray did not deny that he had come to visit him as an emissary from the Lord Chancellor himself; he had in fact breakfasted in his lordship's company that morning. Here evidently was an opportunity to extricate himself from the whole unhappy business. Hamilton Rowan had on some pre-vious occasion told the Colonel that he regretted "Having come to Ireland when party feeling ran so high." He had indicated that once the prosecution were disposed of he would be all too glad to retire to England. The Colonel had reported this re-mark to the Lord Chancellor and was now empowered by him to say that if Hamilton Rowan would in fact consent to leave Ireland and to have no further connection with Irish politics, then steps would be taken to have the prosecution quashed.

The proffered compromise was indeed tempting. At the very moment when Hamilton Rowan was becoming disgusted with his fellow conspirators, at the very moment when his mother's death had brought him a fortune of £8,000 a year and the prospect of living in affluence with his family in England, this clean slate was offered by the Lord Chancellor himself. Unfortunately, however, Lord Fitzgibbon attached to his offer the condition that Hamilton Rowan should publicly sever all connection with the United Irishmen. Such a renouncement would affect his honour. He refused in any manner to repudiate his associates. The offer came to nothing and from that moment Hamilton Rowan was linked irretrievably to a bitter chain of circumstance.

Drennan, who had watched these negotiations with some anxiety was apprehensive lest Hamilton Rowan might give way. "Rowan," he writes, "was quite down today. He has personal but, between ourselves, no political courage. The disputes between him and his wife are most outrageously violent, often on the brink of separation, yet she still gains something and has an insurmountable obstinacy." Drennan could not conceal his delight when Hamilton Rowan eventually rejected Lord Fitzgibbon's offer. "He has extricated himself," he wrote to McTier, "with honour. . . . I think Rowan has shown that the old age of chivalry has not passed away."

In the interval an event of great importance had occurred. On February 1, 1793, the French National Convention declared war upon England. The United Irishmen were faced with a crucial decision. It was no longer a question of agitating for Catholic Emancipation or for electoral reforms. A more decisive issue had been joined. Hamilton Rowan's loyalty to his associates had already driven him into the ranks of the extremists; he might well have taken his wife's advice and chosen this occasion to break without dishonour from the associations of the past; he failed to do so. He had always, as Drennan was at last beginning to notice, been fatally subject to fresh influences. At this crucial moment of his life he was exposed to an influence more potent, since more congenial, than that of Tone himself. It was in the early months of 1793 that he first came into touch with Lord Edward Fitzgerald.

# VII

## TRIAL AND IMPRISONMENT, 1794

Lord Edward Fitzgerald–Drennan's anxieties–Secret negotiations
with the French Committee of Public Safety–Hamilton Rowan's
visit to Edinburgh–He challenges the Lord Advocate to a duel–
His triumphant return to Belfast–Jack Giffard—Hamilton Rowan's
trial–Curran's speech–Lord Clonmell's summing up–His sentence–
Imprisonment in Newgate.

## (1)

IT IS not surprising that Hamilton Rowan should have been
overwhelmed from the outset by this romantic personality.
At the very moment when he was beginning to doubt the
integrity and courage of his own associates; when he was
beginning to doubt whether he had in fact been wise to sacrifice his friends, his family and his fortune to an idea which
was already a trifle musty; when the charm of the American
and French Revolutions was beginning to grow dim; and
when he was considering whether on the whole it would not
be possible to make his peace with the Government and to
extricate himself from a situation which was daily becoming
more dangerous and false; at that very moment he was con-
fronted with a younger man, nurtured in similar traditions,
fired by the same hatreds and passions, and determined at
whatever cost to pursue his theory to the end. It is not surprising that the embers of Hamilton Rowan's enthusiasm
which had been damped by his wife's objurgations and by the
dead weeds of continuous disillusion should once again have
crackled into fire at the fresh wind of energy which Fitzgerald
brought with him.

Fitzgerald was at the time twenty-nine years of age. He also had had his failures and his disappointments. He had fought well in the American War but his prowess had gone unrewarded. His devotion to his cousin Charles James Fox, his passion for the French Revolution, had only the year before driven him to Paris. He had spent his days there in the company of Thomas Paine. He had in fact attended the banquet at White's Hotel, in the Passage des Petits Pères, when under Paine's guidance the English friends of the Revolution had sent an address to the French National Convention trusting that "the armies of liberty will not lay down their arms until tyrants and slaves are no more." He had been cashiered for his part in these proceedings and had just arrived in Dublin, fired by a sense of ill usage, and bringing with him his young and vivacious wife Pamela, the reputed daughter of Philippe Egalité and Madame de Genlis. Pamela was ill received by Dublin society and the indignation of her young husband knew no bounds. Only six days after his arrival he took his seat as Member for Kildare and attacked the administration and the Lord Lieutenant as "the worst subjects the King has." Hamilton Rowan was delighted by this outburst. He walked round to Leinster House and left his card upon Lord Edward Fitzgerald. The acquaintance thus formed rapidly developed into intimacy, and the gay Parisian laughter of Pamela was often heard in the drawing-room at Dominick Street.

Drennan was not quite sure whether he approved of the intrusion into their intimate circle of Lord Edward Fitzgerald. He met him early in 1793 dining at Dominick Street. "A lovely faced youth," he calls him, but there is a note of caution in his eulogy. "He was," he writes to his brother-in-law in Belfast, "plain and familiar in his manners as in his dress. Not too talkative, seems honest, zealous and republican. All his thoughts bend to France. Uncautious, unreserved; wished to know much about the North; was but half satisfied at our declaration of its avowed coincidence with King, Lords and Commons. He said that Paine had nearly a design to come over here. We thought that at present he would do more harm than good. He said there would be war. Chauvelin had assured him that there would and if there would there would be a landing. We hoped that Parliament would intercept that by giving the reform that would satisfy the people. He said they would never please the people and that it was impossible they could. In short, my dear Sam, I believe that he is a noble emissary from France, but an incautious one, and I fear he will be entrapped by some of our state inquisitors. However as the Leinster family are by nature capricious, he may probably be soon diluted here."

He was not diluted, and Drennan observed with anxiety Hamilton Rowan's increasing subservience to Fitzgerald's passionate ideas. He records sadly that Hamilton Rowan "has evidently fallen in love with Lord Edward Fitzgerald." He records with some relief that the Duke of Leinster, "with the utmost indignation," had forbidden his brother to join the United Irishmen. And indeed the Society, having been driven to extremes, was rapidly becoming more seditious and indiscreet. Keogh, the Chairman of the Catholic Committee, who attended one of their meetings at this date was even more alarmed. He was furious with their careless habit of admitting casual strangers to their meetings. "Dick," he said to Richard McCormack, "men's lives are not safe with fellows who would act in this manner." Assuredly men's lives were not safe. The inner ring of the United Irishmen consisted at this time of 39 Protestants of whom 8 died on the gallows, 45 Presbyterians of whom 9 died on the gallows, and 42 Catholics of whom 17 died on the gallows.

Nor was William Drennan so far wrong when he guessed that Fitzgerald, and with him Hamilton Rowan, were gradually being entangled in a dangerous connection with the Revolutionary Government of France. From the very first the Committee of Public Safety had had hopes of an Irish Insurrection in the event of war with England and had, some years before, sent over Rabaud de St. Etienne upon a preliminary visit of inspection.  When in Paris in 1792 Lord Edward Fitzgerald had assured Thomas Paine that if the French could land an expeditionary force of only 4,000 men upon the coast of Ireland the whole country would rise in their support. Paine repeated the remark to Lebrun of the Committee of National Safety.  The latter decided to send over to Ireland an American of the name of Oswald to make a report.  Colonel Oswald arrived in Dublin in June 1793.  Tone, to whom he had been recommended, was too cautious to see him.  Hamilton Rowan was less discreet; he saw Oswald and gave him particulars regarding the present state of Ireland.  As was inevitable this interview was reported to Dublin Castle.  The attitude of the authorities towards Hamilton Rowan became increasingly hostile.  He confirmed their worst suspicions by an ill-advised journey which at this delicate moment he paid to Edinburgh.

(2)

The revolutionary fervour which after 1789 spread throughout Europe had led to the formation in London of the "Society of the Friends of the People."  In October 1792, under the chairmanship of the Scottish nationalist Thomas Muir, a meeting of the Society was held in Glasgow for the purpose of founding a kindred society in Scotland.  Hamilton Rowan, hearing of this meeting, had addressed to them on behalf of the United Irishmen a letter couched in the usual revolutionary language.  In this letter, while expressing the hope that the tyranny of governments would not "drive the people into republicanism" he welcomed the fact that "the spirit of freedom moves on the face of Scotland, and that light seems to break upon the chaos of her internal government."  The Scottish audience were somewhat shocked by this pronouncement but Muir thereafter crossed to Dublin where he was warmly entertained by the United Irishmen.  On his return to Scotland he was arrested for sedition, victimized by a trail which was so shocking that it outraged Lord Romilly who happened to be present as a spectator, and transported to Botany Bay. After many adventures he escaped to France where he eventually died of a wound received on his voyage.

During the course of Muir's infamous trial the Lord Advocate (Dundas) read out to the jury some letters from Hamilton Rowan, whom he described as "one of those wretches who had fled from the justice of their country." He also, much to Hamilton Rowan's indignation, described the seal of the United Irishmen as representing "a human heart pierced by a spear" whereas in fact, clumsy though it was, it portrayed the cap of liberty mounted upon a pike. Hamilton Rowan once again became convinced that his honour had been called in question. He wrote to the Lord Advocate asking him whether he had in fact employed these obnoxious expressions. Receiving no reply he decided to exact satisfaction in person. Accompanied by Simon Butler he crossed to Scotland in October 1793 and arrived at Edinburgh on November 4. He was at once arrested but released on bail offered by Colonel Norman McLeod. On the next day he visited the Advocate General who informed him that he did not consider himself accountable to Hamilton Rowan or to any other person for any observations which in the course of his official duty he felt it proper to make. Rowan and Butler appear to have been fully satisfied by this curt negative and returned in triumph to Dumbreck's hotel. They were entertained that evening by a banquet at the Hunter's Tavern and on their return to Belfast they were, according to the "History of Belfast," welcomed by a "select party" and "elegantly entertained at dinner." "That evening," so writes the Belfast historian, "was spent with that conviviality and heartfelt pleasure which the patriotic and the virtuous alone experience."

It is difficult to understand why this apparently pointless and ineffective expedition should have created such a sensation. Mrs. Hamilton Rowan, for her part, was convinced that the English Government were anxious by this device to lure

Hamilton Rowan to Scotland in the hope that he could thus be implicated in Thomas Muir's seditious activities, convicted by an amenable Scottish jury, and sent off from there to Botany Bay.  If such a plan existed, it was indeed a bold act on Hamilton Rowan's part to put his head within the lion's mouth, and it may well be that anxiety regarding his escapade and relief at his return explains the jubilation with which he was received in Belfast.  That the incident gained him further publicity is certain.  The Dublin newspapers were full of the event and published a long letter from Hamilton Rowan pointing out, that by his return to Ireland to surrender to his bail, he had proved the Lord Advocate's assertion to be a "falsehood." He was also depicted in "Kay's Caricatures" as walking in Edinburgh in the company of Simon Butler.  According to the caption attached to this caricature he "walked with an air of nonchalance."  The club which he carried was inscribed with the words "A pill for a puppy."

I have the impression that my great-great-grandfather at this period was not at his best.

## (3)

It may possibly be true, as Hamilton Rowan and his friends asserted and believed, that the Irish Government postponed his trial until Jack Giffard became sheriff and they could count upon him to provide a jury who would return the verdict which they desired.  Giffard was not an estimable man.  As editor of the "Dublin Journal" he was generally regarded as in the pay of the authorities but his animosity against the United Irishmen may have been based upon more reputable convictions.  Jonah Barrington refers to his "detestation of the Pope and his adoration of King William" on each of which subjects he was "occasionally delirious."  He had on one occasion been the victim of one of Curran's most devastating attacks.  Curran had called him "The hired traducer of his country, the excommunicated of his fellow citizens, the regal rebel, the unpunished ruffian, the bigoted agitator! In the city a firebrand, in the court a liar, in the streets a bully, in the field a coward! And so obnoxious is he to the very party he would espouse that he is only supportable by doing those acts which the less vile refuse to execute." Giffard was so thunderstruck by this onslaught that he could find no rejoinder more apposite than "I could spit upon you in the desert."

In any case when Giffard had been sheriff for three months and the necessary jury had been empanelled, Hamilton Rowan was summoned to the Court of King's Bench. His trial opened on Wednesday, January 19, 1794, before the Lord Chief Justice Lord Clonmell. The Attorney General and the Solicitor General appeared for the prosecution. Hamilton Rowan had engaged Curran for his defence.

The Attorney General in opening the case for the prosecution began by accusing the United Irishmen of having used the Volunteers for the purpose of terrorizing the Administration. "That sacred name," he said, "was made a cloak for arming banditti." He recalled the formation of the National Guard "with clothing of a particular uniform, with emblems of harps divested of the royal crown." He reminded the jury of the proclamation forbidding armed assemblies and then proceeded in detail to describe the scene in Pardon's fencing room. He read to them, paragraph by paragraph, the unfortunate pamphlet which Drennan had drafted and which Hamilton Rowan was accused of distributing. "You will perceive," he sneered, "in his publication the frippery of the French language as now used." He begged them to consider the matter objectively. Could any sober man question that the meeting in Cope Street, the wording and the distribution of the pamphlet, were calculated "to raise discontents against the government, to disturb the people and to overawe the Parliament"?

Two witnesses had been procured for the prosecution. The first was Lieutenant John Lyster of the British army who asserted upon oath that he had seen Hamilton Rowan actually handle and distribute the pamphlet. The second was William Morton who averred the same but admitted on cross-examination that he had been unable clearly to watch the proceedings, since one of the beams of the fencing hall obstructed a full view from the gallery. Witnesses for the defence were called to throw doubt upon the reliability of John Lyster who in fact appears to have been an untrustworthy person who was subsequently cashiered.

Curran then rose to make his speech for the defence. It was regarded at the time, and is still regarded, as a masterpiece of forensic eloquence. He stood there stockily, his black eyes flashing with fire, his heavy under lip protruding with pugnacity. The Sheriff Giffard gave an order and a platoon of soldiers filed into the court, distributing themselves at key points in the public gallery, their uniforms detaching themselves like scarlet exclamation marks against the drab excited crowd. Their entry gave Curran a cue for his opening remarks. It also enabled him to have a lunge at his old enemy Giffard, whom he described as "a corpse floating up to the surface merely from Putrefaction." Was this in fact a civil trial when the military had to be called in to check in advance the "throb of public anxiety which beats from one end to the other of this hall"? Was it in such an atmosphere that a jury could decide the fate of a fellow citizen? Why, he asked, had the administration not dared to bring this case before a Grand Jury? Why had the case been brought forward in the ungracious form of an ex-officio Information? Why in spite of the insistent demands of the accused that he should be granted an early trial had the case been postponed for all these months? "I beg you," he thundered to the jury, "I beg you to consider whether this man is being pursued as a criminal or hunted down as a victim."

Was it in fact a crime to suggest a reform of the electoral System? Was it so dreadful to suggest that "three million of the inhabitants of this country, whose whole number is but four, should be admitted to an efficient situation in the State"?

The pamphlet, it is true, had used the phrase "Universal Emancipation." But was that phrase in fact so very horrible? Curran paused and then, gathering all his fierce energy together, launched out into an impassioned passage which, in spite of the soldiers dotted uneasily in their midst, brought thunders of applause from the gallery:

"Do you think it wise or humane, at this moment, to insult the Catholics by sticking up in the pillory the man who dared to stand forth as their advocate? I put it to your oaths; do you think that a blessing of that kind, that a victory obtained by justice over bigotry and oppression, should have a stigma cast upon it by an ignominious sentence upon men bold and honest enough to propose that measure? To propose the redeeming of religion from the abuses of the Church, the reclaiming of three millions of men from bondage, and giving liberty to all who had the right to demand it? Giving I say, in the so much censured words of this paper, giving 'UNIVERSAL EMANCIPATION.'

"I speak in the spirit of British law, which makes liberty commensurate with and inseparable from British soil—which proclaims even to the stranger and the sojourner, the moment he sets foot upon British soil, that the ground upon which he treads is holy, and consecrated by the genius of UNIVERSAL EMANCIPATION.

"No matter in what language his doom may have been pronounced—no matter what complexion incompatible with freedom an Indian or an African sun may have burnt upon him—no matter in what disastrous battle his liberty may have been cloven down— no matter with what solemnities he may have been devoted upon the altar of slavery—the first moment he touches the sacred soil of Britain the altar and the god sink together in the dust; his soul walks abroad in her own majesty, his body swells beyond the measure of the chains which burst around him, and he stands redeemed, regenerated and disenthralled, by the irresistible genius of UNIVERSAL EMANCIPATION."

Yet even if it were a crime thus publicly to affirm the principles of British Law, had the Crown proved that Hamilton Rowan had in fact distributed the pamphlet? The witness

Morton had admitted that he could not see what actually happened; the witness Lyster was obviously not to be trusted. Could the jury really believe that a man such as Hamilton Rowan, a man of the "most beloved personal character, of one of the most respected families of the country," could in fact become a danger to the State? "Not to be acquainted with Mr. Hamilton Rowan," said Curran, "is want of personal good fortune." Was it likely that such a man "could apostatize from every principle that could bind him to the State—his birth, his property, his education, his character and his children? Are these the materials of which we suppose anarchy and public rapine to be formed?"

"I will not relinquish," concluded Curran, "the confidence that this day will be the period of his sufferings; and however mercilessly he has been hitherto pursued, that your verdict will send him home to the arms of his family and the wishes of his people. But if (which Heaven forbid) it hath still been unfortunately determined that, because he was not bent to power and authority, because he would not bow down before the golden calf and worship it, he is to be bound and cast into the furnace; I do trust in God that there is a redeeming spirit in the constitution which shall be seen to walk with the sufferer through the flame, and to preserve him unhurt through the conflagration."

The Lord Chief Justice, in summing up, instructed the jury to return a verdict finding Hamilton Rowan guilty of "endeavouring by tumult and by force to make alterations in the constitution and the government and overturn them both." Lord Clonmell, in after life, was ashamed of his conduct of this trial and refused to have it mentioned in his presence. Yet in fairness to the administration it must be admitted that they knew all about Hamilton Rowan's conversations with Colonel Oswald and that they could, had they been vindictive, have prosecuted him there and then for High Treason. Lord Clonmell, that shy and convivial man of the world—"half liked, half reprobated; too high to be despised, too low to be respected"—preferred a lesser irregularity to a sentence of death. The jury within ten minutes returned a verdict of guilty. Lord Clonmell reserved the sentence, hoping doubtless that public excitement would calm down. Hamilton Rowan was removed to Newgate escorted by troops and followed by a murmuring crowd.

On Friday, September 7, 1794, the prisoner was brought from Newgate to hear his sentence. He asked to say a few words. "I avow myself," he said, "to be a United Irishman; I glory in the name." On joining the Society he had taken the oath "to seek the emancipation of every class of my fellow citizens." He had fulfilled that oath. In so far as the pamphlet was concerned, "I honour," he said, "the head that conceived it and I love the hand that penned it." "I ask," he concluded, "no favour, but I submit myself to the clemency and justice of the Court, and I trust that whatever may be their sentence I shall bear it with becoming fortitude."

He was then sentenced to two years' imprisonment and to a fine of five hundred pounds. In addition he was to give security for good conduct to the amount of £4,000 and for a period of seven years.

## (4)

The excitement in Dublin was intense. Hamilton Rowan himself managed to escape notice. "The crowds around the court-house," he records, "were so irritated that for fear of mischief I stole out of the Court by the back-door, accompanied by Sheriff Jenkins, and was by him lodged in prison immediately upon sentence being pronounced." Curran, however, was immediately recognized and the crowd flocked around him. He made them a short speech to the effect that every method should be taken to bring perjured witnesses to punishment. So stimulated were they by this remark that they took the lamps from Lady Clonmell's carriage and by their light carried Curran shoulder-high to his home. Apart from this dem-

onstration there was no disturbance or riot. Dublin settled
down to sleep.

Hamilton Rowan had asked that he might serve his sentence
at the jail in Naas. This request was not unnaturally refused.
His friends hoped to have him transferred to Kilmainham Jail
"which," Drennan comments, "is a much more roomy place
and where he might in some time come to such good understanding with the gaoler as to ride out when he chose. And
indeed the crowd at Newgate, especially if our Belfast friends
are sent there, will be so great as to form a ground for the
request at least by his counsel, for he himself will not move
in it."

Hamilton Rowan accepted the role of patriot martyr with
some complacency. He had his miniature painted by Cullen
and arranged for an engraving of it to be made for public
consumption. He also conceived the idea of commissioning
another artist to paint a large picture representing "Hamilton
Rowan, his wife, his son and his father, on his first entrance
into Newgate." There is no evidence to show that this commission was ever executed. Meanwhile he busied himself with
writing an account of his own trial which was to be published
by Byrne of Grafton Street. Lord Clonmell, hearing of this
project, became uneasy. He sent for Byrne and glowered at
him terribly. "Take care, Sir," he shouted at him, "what you
do; for if there are any reflections on the judges of the land,
by the eternal God I shall lay you by the heels."

Conditions in Newgate prison were not unbearable. "My
situation in Gaol," he writes in his autobiography, "was not
to be complained of, though I had indeed a small room, and
some of the conveniences particularly necessary in any hab-
itation were most execrable. During the day, visitors were
admitted, my dinner was brought from my own house, and
Mrs. Rowan and two of my children constantly accompanied
it, except on Sunday when I usually invited some of my
fellow prisoners, who were of the better order, to share it
with me."

He was determined not to imitate the conduct of Butler and Boyd who had so shocked the Society of the United Irishmen by the extravagance of their living while in Newgate jail. Their wine bill alone had cost the Society the sum of £500 in the space of two months. Hamilton Rowan, who was afflicted with a tender conscience in regard to what he called "his un-toiled-for affluence," refused to receive any outside assistance. "I will not have any wine," he wrote, "let me have Bristol water and good beer at my meals."

Meanwhile the addresses of condolence poured in upon him. There was an address from the Working Manufacturers of Dublin. There were many letters from England and Scotland. There was, naturally enough, an address from the Society of United Irishmen. "We disdain," they wrote, "to address a mind like yours in the language of pity and condolence. Although torn from what constitutes the chief felicity of your being, the society of an amiable and exemplary wife, and the superintendence of a numerous and promising offspring, you are plunged into a loathsome prison, yet the rectitude of your cause, the firmness of your principles, the unbending energy of your mind, the ardent affection of your grateful countrymen, to the assertion of whose liberties you have devoted yourself, will cheer and sustain you through the progress of a tedious imprisonment." To all these communications Hamilton Rowan returned very suitable replies. The United Irishmen had, with some lack of delicacy, inserted into their address a passage referring to "Hampden, Russell and Sydney, who sealed their principles with their blood." "Do not," Hamilton Rowan replied, "tarnish the memory of the illustrious dead by hasty comparisons with the living. If my sufferings, slight as they are in comparison with past and present examples, shall in any way contribute to our common object, I shall deem myself both honoured and rewarded." He concluded this letter with the motto *"Fais ce que doy, advienne que pourra."*

He was not in fact much to be pitied. He had escaped the

supreme sentence to which his negotiations with Colonel Oswald might have exposed him. He had avoided being exposed
in the pillory, an indignity which Mrs. Hamilton Rowan, Butler and Drennan had so much dreaded. The fine had not
been too heavy nor the term of imprisonment too long. There
was every prospect that if he behaved with discretion his sentence would be reduced and that he would be able, without
dishonour, to retire to England, there to enjoy the esteem of
all liberal minded gentlemen and the amenities of his large
fortune. Meanwhile Newgate and his glorious martyrdom
were not intolerable. "Rowan is hearty and well," records
Drennan in a letter of February 19, "I was with him yester-
day when the Duke of Leinster paid him a second visit along
with Lord Edward. . . ."

The fates, however, had decreed no easy solution. For it
was at this stage that the Reverend William Jackson called at
Newgate.

# VIII

## THE REVEREND WILLIAM
## JACKSON, 1794–1795

The Duchess of Kingston–Her dispute with Samuel Foote–She employs Parson Jackson and the attorney Cokayne–Jackson visits Dublin on a secret mission from the French Government–He meets Leonard MacNally–He is introduced to Hamilton Rowan in Prison–Tone is persuaded to write a secret memorandum on the state of Ireland–Hamilton Rowan copies this memorandum and gives it to Jackson–Cokayne warns the Government and the document is intercepted–Tone makes a "compromise" with the authorities–Jackson is arrested–His trial and death.

### (1)

ELIZABETH CHUDLEIGH, maid of honour to the Princess of Wales, had in 1744 been secretly married to Augustus Harvey, subsequently Earl of Bristol. She thereafter became the mistress of the Duke of Kingston whom she married while her first husband was still alive. The Duke died a year later bequeathing his entire fortune to his reputed widow. His natural heirs were incensed by this procedure and an indictment for bigamy was filed against the Duchess. She was tried by the House of Lords and found guilty. Among the penalties prescribed by law for this offence was that of being branded as a bigamist upon the palm of the hand. Elizabeth Chudleigh evaded this indignity by pleading that, although assuredly not the Duchess of Kingston, she was certainly the Countess of Bristol, and as such a peeress of the realm. Being a woman of determination she thereupon sailed from England in her yacht, was well received by Catherine II at St. Petersburg, and purchased a large estate in the neighborhood of the Russian capital which she christened Chudleigh." She established a profitable brandy distillery on her estate but after some years she wearied of Russia and returned to Paris where she died.

When the Duchess of Kingston's scandal was at its height the dramatist Samuel Foote lampooned her in a play entitled *A trip to Calais* and in the character of "Kitty Crocodile." The Duchess still possessed sufficient influence to persuade the Lord Chamberlain to ban the play, and a correspondence of extreme virulence ensued between her and Samuel Foote, copies of which the latter would send to the public newspapers in which they were published with glee. Feeling that she was getting the worst of the controversy, the Duchess of Kingston called to her assistance two men who were destined to have a disastrous effect upon the fortunes of Hamilton Rowan. The first was a seedy attorney of the name of Cokayne. The second was a clergyman of Irish extraction of the name of William Jackson. "Pray Madam," wrote Foote in one of his open letters to the Duchess, "is not J——n the name of your female confidential secretary? May you never want the benefit of clergy in every emergency." Jackson at the time was editor of *The Daily Ledger* and curate at St. Mary-le-Strand. Under his direction the Duchess's letters to Foote became more and more scurrilous. Foote replied by writing *The Capuchin* in which Jackson was lampooned in the character of "Dr. Viper." Jackson retorted by circulating a salacious attack upon Foote using the pseudonym of Humphrey Nettle. He then suborned a groom, who had been discharged from Foote's service, to accuse his former master of immoral practices. Foote was acquitted, but the proceedings did much to damage his reputation and his hitherto unbroken success. Jackson became editor of the *Morning Post,* and was thereafter sent by Mr. Pitt to Paris to collect information during the uncertain interval between the deposition of Louis XVI and his trial. While in Paris he came into contact with Nicholas Madgett, an Irishman employed in the French Ministry of Foreign Affairs. Madgett induced him to transfer his services from the English Government to the French Government and to undertake a secret mission on behalf of the Committee of Public Safety. He was to report upon the number and quality of the English troops in Ireland and to ascertain to what extent the Irish patriots and peasantry would support a French invasion. While in London he was to act through a Mr. William Stone, a coal-merchant, whose brother, John Hurford Stone, was prominent among the English Jacobins of Paris and a partner of the Reverend Benjamin Beresford who has already figured in this story.

Jackson travelled to England via Hamburg and hid himself in a hotel in Bloomsbury. The intoxicants of the French Revolution appear to have deprived him of all sense of reticence as of all judgment of political realities. He induced Mr. Stone to sound Pitt's political opponents, and among them Lord Lauderdale and Richard Brinsley Sheridan, who, as might have been expected, were horrified by his proposals. He also saw much of his old crony of the Duchess of Kingston days, the attorney Cokayne, to whom with amazing indiscretion he confided the purpose of his mission. Cokayne crept round to Downing Street and told the whole story to Mr. Pitt. He was instructed to simulate great sympathy for Parson Jackson's ideas and purposes, to accompany him to Ireland, and to report to the British Government his every movement, action and association. If he performed his task properly he would receive, not only the moneys which Parson Jackson owed him, but a pension for life.

The pair of them arrived in Dublin on April 1, 1794.

(2)

One of the most trusted members in the inner circle of the United Irishmen was a barrister of the name of Leonard Mac-Nally. He was an original member of the Dublin branch of the Society, had been counsel for Napper Tandy and had published many rebellious verses in the organ of the movement, *The Northern Star*. He was not prepossessing in appearance since, although his dark eyes burned with patriotic fervour, yet one leg was shorter than the other, he had lost a thumb and his face was such "as no washing could clean." His house in Dublin became the meeting place for all the more determined conspirators, and when trouble came it was always to MacNally's eloquence and forensic capacity that the United Irishmen had recourse. His name figures in all the more famous state trials of the period; it was he who defended Parson Jackson when the moment came: it was he who spoke so eloquently in defence of the Catholic patriots that he drew tears from Curran's eyes; it was he who defended Robert Emmet with such passionate intensity, who wailed aloud at the tragedy of Emmet's conviction, and who prayed with him in prison on the very morning of his execution.

Only much later was it discovered that all this time Mac-Nally had been drawing a pension of £300 a year from Dublin Castle; that of all the spies and informers whom they employed it was he who provided them with the most rapid and detailed particulars; that it was he who first denounced Lord Edward Fitzgerald and who received an extra payment of £200 for his betrayal of Emmet; and that it was his custom, when defending the rebels, to send an advance copy of his brief to the Attorney General. All this, however, did not transpire until long after MacNally and his several victims were dead. In 1794 he was still regarded as a man in whom the utmost confidence could be placed. And it was at dinner in his house that Parson Jackson and Cokayne were first introduced to the United Irishmen.

Among the guests at this dinner party were Simon Butler and a Catholic solicitor of the name of Edward Lewins, who was in the employment of the firm that was acting for Hamilton Rowan. They spoke of the prospects of a French invasion. Simon Butler doubted whether the peasantry would rise. Cokayne, as was his habit, pretended to take but little interest in the conversation. He left the table, sat in a distant armchair, placed his hand across his eyes and conveyed the impression of being in a profound slumber. The butler, however, in passing round the table observed that he was in fact listening intently; he whispered to MacNally "to be careful of the gentleman in the corner; he had noticed his eyes glinting through his fingers." Nothing further was decided at that dinner party, except that Lewins agreed to arrange for Parson Jackson to visit Hamilton Rowan in Newgate.

Among the letters which Jackson had brought with him was one from Madgett to Lord Edward Fitzgerald. In a manuscript note in his copy of MacNeven's *Pieces of Irish History* Hamilton Rowan wrote the words "Lord Edward declined to have any conversation with Jackson." It may have been that Lord Edward suspected Jackson of being an English spy. It may also have been, as Senator MacDermot suggests in his admirable biography of Theobald Wolfe Tone, that he was feeling sore at the moment with the Committee of Public Safety who had guillotined his father-in-law Philippe Egalité in the previous November. Hamilton Rowan in any case had no hesitation in seeing Jackson and discussing with him the purpose of his mission to Dublin. The idea occurred to him that Theobald Wolfe Tone would be the very man to provide Jackson with the information he wanted. He wrote to Tone asking him to call upon Jackson at Hyde's Coffee House in Dame Street. Tone did so on April 12. He seems from the very first to have derived the impression that Jackson was unreliable and to have desired to keep aloof from the whole business. Two days later, however, when Tone was paying his daily visit to Hamilton Rowan in prison, Jackson and Cokayne were introduced. In his subsequent confession Tone stated that he had retired into a corner of the room with Cokayne where they had discussed the difficulties of Irish travel and the poorness of the accommodation offered to travellers. Jackson and Hamilton Rowan held a whispered conversation in the other corner. The latter beckoned Tone to join them which he did. Cokayne remained aloof. Hamilton Rowan then told Tone that he and Jackson had been talking about the condition of

Ireland and that Jackson had asserted that if the French Government knew the full facts, "they would certainly afford every assistance to enable the Irish to assert their independence." Tone, according to his own statement, remarked that this would be "a most severe and grievous remedy for our abuses" but that he saw no other. On the next day Hamilton Rowan asked Tone to draw up a memorandum which could be sent to the Committee of Public Safety. On April 16 Tone called again at Newgate, found Jackson and Cokayne in Hamilton Rowan's room, and showed them the paper he had prepared. Jackson asked if he might have the memorandum Tone had written, and the latter gave it him. A few minutes later, however, regretting this indiscretion, he asked for the paper back. He then handed the paper to Hamilton Rowan telling him to burn it, but adding that he might have a copy of it if he wished. Tone thereafter went down to Drogheda to attend, on behalf of the Catholic Committee, the trial of two Catholics arrested for sedition.

Tone returned to Dublin on April 24, called upon Hamilton Rowan at Newgate, and discovered to his "unspeakable astonishment and vexation" that although Hamilton Rowan had burned the original memorandum which Tone had written, he had not merely made two or three copies of it in his own handwriting, but had given these copies to Jackson. From that moment, Tone asserts, he decided to "withdraw himself from a business wherein he saw such grievous indiscretion."

## (3)

The paper which Tone had drafted, and which Hamilton Rowan had copied in his own handwriting and given to Jackson, was in fact a very damning document. It informed the Committee of Public Safety that of a total population of 4,500,000 only 450,000 or one tenth, were identified with the English ascendancy. The "great bulk of the people would probably throw off the yoke, if they saw any force in the country sufficiently strong to resort to for defence." The Dissenters (the number of which Tone gave as 900,000) would join the French "from reason and reflection"; the 3,150,000 Catholics would join them "from hatred of the English name." "The force necessary," concluded the memorandum, "may be not more than twenty thousand and not less than ten thousand men. Supposing them ten thousand, seven thousand should land in the west, and having secured and fortified the landing place, should advance into the middle of the country; at the same time three thousand should land immediately at the capital, and seize on all stores and such persons as might be troublesome. In that event the north would rise to a man, and so having possession of three fourths of the country and the capital, the remaining port, were it so inclined, could make no resistance."

On leaving Newgate Jackson and Cokayne returned to their coffee house in Dame Street. Jackson wrote four letters, one to Stone, one to Benjamin Beresford, and two to Madgett. The latter two were addressed under cover of commercial houses in Amsterdam and Hamburg and purported to deal with purely business matters. They did, however, contain the copies of Tone's memorandum which Hamilton Rowan had written out in his own hand. Jackson posted these letters in the Dublin Post Office. Cokayne had time to warn the authorities that the evidence they required was now in their hands. The letters were intercepted and taken to Dublin Castle.

It is clear from the reports which during those anxious days Cokayne had been sending to Mr. Pitt, some of which Senator MacDermot unearthed among the Chatham Papers in the Record Office, that things had not turned out according to the plan which Cokayne had conceived. He had not enjoyed his association with Parson Jackson, since the latter's habits were not in accordance with his own. Writing to Pitt at 7.30 on the morning of April 18 he had complained that "I can have no other safe time to correspond as he (Jackson) never permitted me to go to bed before two in the morning or without having at least three bottles of claret—a mode so different from my living in London where a pint of wine is my stint that I scarcely go through it; besides the expense is enormous." In spite of this, however, it is evident that Cokayne had no desire to bring his friend to the gallows. What he had hoped would happen was that some emissary, either Tone or Drennan, would be sent to France on behalf of the United Irishmen; that he would be able to give the English Government due warning of this emissary's departure and enable them to arrest him with the incriminating papers upon him. This scheme failed because Wolfe Tone was too wary, and Drennan too timid, to undertake the mission. "I must," he wrote to Pitt, "again repeat and urge to your most serious consideration the abandonment of any thought of molesting Jackson's person." He warned them that if Jackson were "molested" the French Government would certainly exact reprisals against one of the many English prisoners in their possession. This was no idle threat. Hamilton Rowan learnt afterwards that the Committee of Public Safety had warned the British Government through the Russian Ambassador that if Jackson were executed they would take reprisals against General O'Hara who had been captured at Toulon.

The authorities in Dublin hesitated for a few days as to the course of action to pursue. Towards Tone they behaved with a leniency which has much disconcerted his admirers. They were most anxious to obtain his evidence against Jackson and Hamilton Rowan. "The Lord Lieutenant and others," wrote Marcus Beresford to his father on April 28, 1794, "wish me to see Tone and to endeavour to prevail upon him. They will save him and enable him to retire and live elsewhere." Writing on May 1 he adds, "Tone wishes to make reparation for his past conduct by giving such information to Government as might be useful, provided he is not called upon to accuse Hamilton Rowan etc. He did not wish to appear as a witness in a public court." A few days later he wrote, "Tone has withdrawn himself from Dublin by my directions. He will come up whenever I send for him." Tone thus entered into a "compromise" with the Government and his confession is dated May 3. He remained at liberty and was, as will be seen, allowed to leave for America unmolested early in the following year.

Jackson, having completed his business in Dublin, decided that before returning to Paris he would visit Cork in order to examine local conditions and possibly also to buy stores for the French fleet. He had planned to leave Dublin on April 28. But on the morning of that day, while still in bed at Hyde's Coffee House, he was arrested and lodged in Newgate.

Cokayne returned to London and was granted for his services a pension of £250 a year. He thereafter vanishes from the pages of history except for a brief and painful appearance in Charles Phillipps's *Curran and his Contemporaries*. One day in 1822 Phillipps was visited in his chambers in the Temple by "a tall and venerable figure who lingered and hesitated and seemed as if doubtful what to do." Phillipps asked him his name and business. He confessed that he was Cokayne of the Jackson case. Phillipps told him exactly what he thought of paid informers who betrayed their friends. "He uttered not a syllable and left the room."

## (4)

Before I relate the effect of these events upon the fortunes of Hamilton Rowan I shall anticipate my narrative for a page or two in order to recount the tragic end of Parson Jackson. His trial did not take place till April 23, 1795, and, as was inevitable, he was convicted of high treason. A few days later he was driven from Newgate to the court to receive sentence of death. Before leaving his cell he had been visited by his wife who with her own hands prepared for him a cup of tea into which, while the jailer's eyes were averted, he poured a strong dose of arsenic. The scene which followed is vividly described by William Curran in the life of his father.

MacLellan, Jackson's advocate, on his way to the court that

morning was accosted by a friend who said of him: "I have just
seen your client drive by on the way to King's Beach to receive
sentence.  I always said he was a coward and I find I was not
mistaken.  His fears have made him sick—as the coach drove
by I observed him with his head out of the window vomiting
violently."  MacLellan hurried into the court room where he
found Jackson supporting himself against the dock.  "His
frame was in a state of violent perturbation but his mind was
collected."  He beckoned to MacLellan and gasped out the
words, "We have deceived the Senate."  There followed a
pause due to some legal technicality and then the Attorney
General called upon the court to pronounce sentence.  "Accordingly," records William Curran, "the Reverend William
Jackson was set forward and presented a spectacle equally
shocking and affecting.  His body was in a state of profuse
perspiration; when his hat was removed, a dense steam was
seen to ascend from his head and temples; minute and irregu-
lar movements of convulsion were passing to and fro upon
his countenance; his eyes were nearly closed, and when at
intervals they opened, discovered by the glare of death upon
them that the hour of dissolution was at hand.  When called
upon to stand up before the court, he collected the remnant of
his force to hold himself erect; but the attempt was tottering
and imperfect; he stood rocking from side to side with his
arms in the attitude of firmness crossed over his breast, and
his countenance strained by a last proud effort into an expression of elaborate composure.  In this condition he faced
all the anger of the offended law and the more confounding
gazes of the assembled crowd.  The clerk of the crown now
ordered him to hold up his right hand.  He disentangled it
from the other and held it up, but it instantly dropped again.
. . . Mr. Curran rose and addressed some argument to the
court in arrest of judgment.  A legal discussion of considerable length ensued.  The condition of Mr. Jackson was all the
while becoming worse.  Mr. Curran proposed that he should
be remanded as he was in a state of body which rendered any

communication between him and his counsel impracticable. Lord Clonmell thought it lenity to the prisoner to dispose of the question as soon as possible. The windows of the court were thrown open to relieve him and the discussion was renewed; but the fatal group of death tokens were now collecting around him; he was evidently in the final agony. At length, while Mr. Ponsonby, who followed Mr. Curran was urging further reasons for arresting the judgment, the client sunk in the dock."

The following discussion then ensued:

LORD CLONMELL. "If the prisoner is in a state of insensibility it is impossible that I can pronounce the judgment of the Court upon him."

Mr. Thomas Kinsley, a member of the jury, said he would go down to him. He accordingly went into the dock and in a short time informed the Court that the prisoner was dying.

By order of the Court Mr. Kinsley was sworn.

LORD CLONMELL. "Are you in any profession?"

MR. KINSLEY. "I am an apothecary."

LORD CLONMELL. "Can you speak with certainty of the state of the prisoner?"

MR. KINSLEY. "I can. I think him on the verge of eternity."

LORD CLONMELL. "Do you think him capable of hearing the judgment?"

MR. KINSLEY. "I do not think he can."

LORD CLONMELL. "Let him be taken away. Take care that in sending him away no mischief is done. Let him be remanded until further order."

The Sheriff then informed the court that the prisoner was dead.

LORD CLONMELL. "Let an inquisition, and a respectable one be held on the body. You should certainly enquire by what means he died."

The body of the Reverend William Jackson remained in the dock all night.

# IX

## ESCAPE, MAY 1794

Cokayne confesses to Hamilton Rowan that the Government have obtained possession of the Tone memorandum and arrested Jackson–Hamilton Rowan realizes his immediate danger and plans to escape–The jailer Dowell–The midnight scene at Dominick Street –Mrs. Sweetman's account–The Sheridan Brothers–Mr. Sweetman's pleasure boat–Hamilton Rowan sails for France–The Clongowes College story–Visit to James Joyce.

## (1)

It was Cokayne himself who first broke to Hamilton Rowan the news that the Government had secured possession of the Tone memorandum and that Jackson had been arrested. Cokayne entered the cell at Newgate mumbling vague excuses; he had been summoned by the Privy Council and had been obliged to confess to knowledge of the letters which had been laid before them; he had in fact told the Privy Council exactly what had occurred; but Hamilton Rowan need have no further fears. Two witnesses were required for any prosecution for high treason and whatever Cokayne himself may or may not have divulged, his evidence would not in itself be sufficient to secure a conviction. Cokayne may have been sincere in giving such assurances; it was true that under English, although not under Irish, law the testimony of two witnesses was in such cases required. In any case Hamilton Rowan had for once no illusion as to the fate which awaited him. He knew that the memorandum would be identified as being in his handwriting and that he would be convicted of high treason and hanged. He saw clearly that his only possible hope was to escape before the jailers at Newgate were aware that a major charge would be preferred against him. Cokayne did not diminish his anxiety by telling him that he had found the Privy Council insistent in their desire that he should testify against Hamilton Rowan: he had in fact "found them very bitter against him." Hamilton Rowan asked him whether if he managed to escape he would injure Jackson's defence. Cokayne assured him that Jackson's position would in no way be affected. It must be recorded to his credit that he did not divulge to his employers that Hamilton Rowan had confessed to him that escape was in his mind. Cokayne thereafter returned to England where he lived upon his pension and his remorse.

The effect of this news flung Hamilton Rowan into a condition bordering upon panic. "Rowan," writes Drennan to Samuel McTier, "was in a state of great perturbation, and what one would call madness. He bid me say he was a baby and a fool, and was led into ruin by his own unguardedness and by some inaccuracy of Tone's. He has no doubt implicated himself with this Jackson, but I believe, or rather suspect, he has a scheme of getting, if possible, to France, and returning as a guide and that there is some army ready for invasion."

During the thirty-six hours that followed Hamilton Rowan planned and plotted how he could escape from Newgate. His wife, who with all her defects of ill-temper and meanness was a courageous woman, assisted him in his scheme. He decided that Dowell, the under jailer, was amenable to suggestion. He invented a story that he was pressed for money and found it necessary to dispose of one of his estates. The intending purchasers had, however, raised objection to his signing the conveyance while in Newgate on the ground that a deed so dated and addressed might not prove of legal validity. Hamilton Rowan explained to Dowell that if only he could visit his own house in Dominick Street for sufficient time to sign a deed bearing a less official address the sale would be completed and his embarrassments relieved. He could arrange for the gentlemen who were to be the other parties to the deed to visit his house secretly after midnight. He promised that he would give Dowell the sum of £100 if he would personally conduct him to Dominick Street and remain there while the deed was signed.

"The next day," runs Hamilton Rowan's narrative, "was the 1st of May. A little before dinner-hour he came and desired me to be ready at midnight. This I immediately communicated to my friend Mat Dowling, who proposed to meet me at that hour on horseback at the end of Sackville Street. We had a Swiss butler who had lived with us some years, to whom I laid open this part of the plan, and I directed a table to be laid out above stairs with wine, etc., etc., in a front two-pair-of-stair room, the door of which commanded a view of the staircase. He was instructed, when we came to the door, to show us upstairs and to say the gentlemen had called but that they would shortly return.

"About midnight Mr. Dowell appeared in the prison, with his sabre and pistols in his girdle, and thence accompanied me to my own house. On our arrival there the servant did as he was instructed. I then sat down with Mr. Dowell to take some refreshment; in the meantime I had prepared the purse with the 100 guineas, which I threw across the table to him, saying I was much better pleased with his having it than Six-and-eightpenny. And here I must record that he put the purse back to me, saying he did not do it for gain; but I remonstrated, and he relented. At this moment I accused myself of my insincerity; but as Godwin describes in Caleb Williams, under somewhat similar circumstances, I was not prepared to 'maintain my sincerity at the expense of a speedy close to my existence.'

"I then said, as we could not remain long absent, if he had no objection, I would step into the back room opposite, where my wife and eldest boy slept. To this he immediately consented; and I desired I might be called when the gentlemen returned. I entered, changed my clothes for those of my herd, who had opportunely come to town that day with a cow for

the children. I then descended from the window by a knotted
rope which was made fast to the bedpost and reached down to
the garden. I went to the stable, took my horse, and rode to
the head of Sackville Street where Mat Dowling had appointed
to meet me. Here I was obliged to wait nearly half an hour
before Dowling appeared. His delay was occasioned by some
friends having called on him to supper; Mat, never being the
first to break up company, was obliged to remain until the party
separated of themselves, lest he should be suspected of being
concerned in my escape. Some of my friends advised my taking my pistols with me; but I had made up my mind not to
be taken alive, so I only put a razor in my pocket. At last
Dowling came up and we set out for the house of Mr. Sweetman, who was a friend of his, and lived on the sea-side at Sutton, near Baldoyle, by whom and his then wife I was received
with the utmost kindness; and in a short time afterwards
Dowling returned home."

Meanwhile Dowell, the under jailer, had remained in the
front room, fingering his hundred-guinea purse, sipping the
port-wine upon the table, and waiting for "the gentlemen"
who were expected to sign the conveyance. As the minutes
passed he began to feel uneasy. He knocked at the door of
the adjoining bedroom and called to his prisoner that time
was pressing. He received only a mumbled reply. He raised
his voice and ordered his prisoner to return to the front room.
There was no answer beyond a rustle of clothes. It was already half past midnight and in increasing dismay Dowell
clamoured for admittance. In the end Mrs. Hamilton Rowan
was forced to open the door. He found a room in some disorder but tenanted only by Mrs. Rowan and young Gawen
William, then a boy of eleven. Seeing the knotted rope still
tied to the bedpost Dowell swore aloud. Mrs. Rowan used
all her efforts to placate, or at least to detain him. She offered
to protect him from the fury of his superiors; she offered to
arrange for his escape to America; she offered him sufficient
money to start life again in the new world. He replied that

"he would far sooner see Hamilton Rowan hanged." He
rushed from the house to raise the hue and cry. By dawn on
May 2 the whole police force of Dublin was mobilized to
search for Hamilton Rowan.

(2)

Mr. John Sweetman was a Catholic and a man of fortune.
He owned a large brewery in Francis Street, Dublin, and he
had married a brewer's daughter. He was one of the few
Catholics of substance who had taken an active part in the
movement for emancipation and was a member of the Dublin
branch of the United Irishmen. He was subsequently involved
in the rebellion of 1798 and spent sixteen years of his life in
exile. He was in no sense a close associate of Hamilton Rowan
and it was for this reason in all probability that his house was
chosen as a safe place of refuge. He lived at some distance
from Dublin city, at Sutton, near Baldoyle, in a little sea-side
house which he had christened "Rosedale."

The story at this stage is taken up by Mrs. Sweetman,
for whose statement of events I am indebted to my cousin
Hans Rowan Hamilton. Mrs. Sweetman's account runs as
follows:

"On May 1, 1794, my late husband, Robert [*sic*] Sweetman,
retired to rest at an early hour. About 1 o'clock, a maid was
wakened by a loud rapping at the hall door. Enquiring who
was there, she was answered by a person who said he wanted
to see Mr. Sweetman. She said he was in bed and could not
be disturbed. After several applications she was prevailed
upon to tell her master. He was much displeased and annoyed
and told her to tell the person he would not see anyone but
to call in the morning. The maid was prevailed upon a third
time to tell her master the business of the applicant was of
great importance and that he had a letter to be delivered in
person. Her master consented and opened the front door
and was surprised at the appearance of his visitor. He was dis-

guised in a fisherman's dress and Mr. Sweetman said he had looked like a robber. Hamilton Rowan told him who he was, also of his escape and threw himself on his mercy. Mr. Sweetman brought him upstairs and Hamilton Rowan was much excited. After a while, he told Mr. Sweetman of his desire to quit the country and that he would give him half of the money he possessed for a boat.

The following morning they set off for Rushkerries and Balybryn to procure a boat. He offered £500 to anyone to fit up a boat for a gentleman here embarrassed. No-one was found to run the risk for double the amount. When they returned unsuccessful, Rowan was much dejected, not knowing what to do. He occupied a small room with a case of pistols, fully determined in case he was discovered to commit suicide."

Sweetman told him he had a pleasure boat if he would risk so small a craft. There was difficulty in procuring trusty men. After a deal of anxiety he procured three staunch fellows, one of the name of Murray [sic]. The men were promised great remuneration for their arduous undertaking and Sweetman went to Dublin to purchase maps, etc. At the time he was on George's Quay a Captain of a revenue cruiser came to the same shop and told him he had orders to keep a look-out for Hamilton Rowan, not suspecting that Sweetman was conniving at his escape. When Rowan was leaving he gave Mr. Sweetman a letter for his wife, directing her to provide for the families of the men employed to navigate the boat. She never complied with that request.

On May 4, 1794, at 4 a.m. Rowan left. Previous to his departure he went on his knees in the drawing room and prayed God would "preserve and deliver him from all harm."

Mrs. Sweetman's account, written more than twenty-two years after the events she describes, is in some respects inaccurate and in some respects incomplete. When, at 1 a.m. on May 2, Hamilton Rowan arrived at "Rosedale" and roused the household of Mr. Sweetman he was not disguised as a

fisherman; he still wore the smock of his cowherd. He was
not alone, since he was accompanied by Mat Dowling, who
knew Sweetman and who only left them when the latter had
promised to take Hamilton Rowan into his house. He did not
have his pistols with him, since he had decided, if found, to
cut his throat with a razor. There are further details which
Mrs. Sweetman omits. When her husband went to Rush to
search for a smuggler's boat to take the refugee to France
he found the whole village in an uproar. The jailer Dowell,
intent upon regaining his escaped prisoner, had descended upon
Rush and was searching the houses of two of Hamilton
Rowan's former fellows in Newgate jail whom he suspected of
having connived at his escape. Being unable to find a boat,
Sweetman, anxious to rid himself of so dangerous a visitor,
had suggested that he should conceal himself somewhere in
Ireland. Hamilton Rowan insisted that he must take a boat
for France, "both on his own and Mr. Jackson's account."
It was then that Sweetman thought of lending Rowan his own
fishing wherry, "a small pleasure boat, neither seaworthy nor
equipped for a channel cruise." It was Sweetman in the end
who found two smugglers, the brothers Denis and Christopher
Sheridan, who were prepared to convey "an embarrassed gentleman" to France. Meanwhile the authorities had distributed leaflets, and posted placards, warning the public of Hamilton Rowan's escape and offering a reward of £2,000 for information leading to his arrest. Half of this sum would be
paid by the Government themselves, £500 by the municipality
of Dublin, and a further £500 by the outraged jailers and their
friends. When Mr. Sweetman brought the two Sheridan
brothers to "Rosedale" to see Hamilton Rowan, the elder of
the two pulled from his pockets one of the leaflets offering a
reward for his apprehension. "It is," he said, "Mr. Hamilton
Rowan we are to take to France?" "Yes," replied Mr. Sweetman, "and here he is." "Never mind," said Christopher. "By
Jesus we shall land him safe." Hamilton Rowan thanked

them for their generosity and remarked that the name "Sheridan" was in fact of good omen.

A third man had to be engaged and with some difficulty the Sheridan brothers found a fellow smuggler of the name of Murphy, who well knew the smaller harbours of northern France. The stores and charts were shipped secretly. Hamilton Rowan expressed his warm thanks to Mr. and Mrs. Sweetman, and before dawn on May 4th they climbed the wall of Kilbarrack graveyard and put to sea with a fair wind.

That night a storm blew up and they were obliged to return and to anchor under the protection of Howth head. A revenue cutter, as it passed them, dropped into the stern of their boat a further proclamation offering £2,000 for Hamilton Rowan's apprehension. The elder Sheridan confessed to Hamilton Rowan that he had not full confidence in Murphy whereas his brother Denis "loved a sup." It was arranged therefore that either Christopher or Hamilton Rowan should be continuously on deck in case Murphy should turn the boat back to Ireland. On the morning of May 5th they made their second start. When off the west coast of England they sighted the whole British fleet sailing westwards. They managed to elude observation and on the morning of the third day they sighted the coast of France.

(3)

I had always assumed that by combining Hamilton Rowan's own account with the subsequent record of Mrs. Sweetman it would be possible to reconstruct in a complete manner the incidents of those fifty-four hours. I must admit, however, that in this closely packed and neatly bound story there is a loose leaf which causes me some bewilderment. There is a persistent legend that at some time between his escape from Dominick Street and his embarkation on Mr. Sweetman's pleasure boat Hamilton Rowan had the foolhardiness to revisit his house at Rathcoffey. This legend is backed by long local tradition and by such circumstantial detail that it is impossible to dismiss it as wholly invented. On the one hand there is no scrap of written evidence to support the story; on the other hand it is more than likely that a man of Hamilton Rowan's impatient character should have become bored by waiting with his Bible and razor in the back room at "Rosedale" and should have conceived it feasible to make a dash to Rathcoffey to collect money and papers and to bid a final farewell to his family and home.

Before closing this chapter I shall recount how I first hit upon this legend, how my investigations led me to an unexpected and unfruitful interview with James Joyce, and how finally I was enabled to discover the origin of the legend and to reproduce it for what it is worth.

One day during the last war I was reading James Joyce's *Portrait of the Artist as a Young Man*. I was reading the book dreamily, as James Joyce should always be read, allowing my imagination to float at ease among the interior monologues of young Stephen Daedalus. Suddenly my attention was arrested by the following phrase: "It would be better to be in the study-hall than out there in the cold. The sky was pale and cold but there were lights in the castle. He wondered from which window Hamilton Rowan had thrown his hat upon the Ha Ha, and had there been flowerbeds at that time under the windows." A few pages further on the name occurred again. "He came out," I read, "on the landing above the entrance hall and looked about him. That was where Hamilton Rowan had passed and the marks of the soldiers' slugs were there. And it was there that the old servants had seen the ghost in the white coat of a marshal."

I was fascinated by these references. James Joyce, I knew, had been educated at Clongowes Wood College which is situated in the neighbourhood of Rathcoffey House. Obviously some incident had occurred involving English soldiery, a hat and a Ha Ha, which was not mentioned in the Autobiography or other records. I decided to ask Joyce the origin of the story but many years passed before I had occasion to see him.

It was in February 1934 that, happening to have an empty day in Paris, I decided to occupy my time by running both Joyce and the Clongowes legend to earth. He was living in retirement at the time, protected against the intrusions of the outer world by an awed phalanx of disciples over whom he exercised a somewhat hierophantic sway. I knew that he had left his house in the Avenue St. Philibert at Passy and I was warned that I should experience some difficulty in eliciting his later address. I therefore presented myself with due reverence at the book shop in the Rue de l'Odéon which I knew to be one of the subsidiary temples of the cult. I was received with real kindliness by Miss Sylvia Beach who not only gave me Joyce's present address in Paris but actually allowed me to use her telephone in order to fix an appointment with the master himself. An audience was arranged for that very evening at No. 42 rue de Galilée where Joyce had been lent a furnished flat.

The door was opened by a large and hearty young man, dressed in an enormous tweed greatcoat, whom I subsequently identified as Joyce's son. I was shown into a dim trim little drawing room with a parquet floor, a few rugs and many occasional chairs and tables in the style of Louis XV. The room had about it the enclosed atmosphere of an unused sitting room in some neat provincial hotel, at Grenoble it might have been, or else at Montelimar. One expected to find upon the central table bound volumes illustrating the châteaux and the other hotels of France. But as I gazed around the room I observed that on each table there were grouped floral tributes, —a mass of decaying narcissus, a huge and horrible vase stuffed with mimosa already turning brown, some cyclamen still gay and upright in a moss-covered basket tied with a large silk ribbon. Evidently the disciples had been celebrating Joyce's birthday on the day before.

As I gazed at these objects I became conscious of sounds in

the flat outside.  Doors closed, feet hurried along passages, and quick whispers reached me from beyond the door.  After a few minutes the son rejoined me, still dressed in his enormous greatcoat, though the little room was hot.  He was not a very articulate young man and the minutes passed heavily.  Suddenly, and very quietly the door opened and Joyce crept into the room.  He turned his sensitive face towards the windows, moving it rapidly from side to side, seeking for the bunched shadow somewhere which would represent his guest.  It was obvious that he had just shaved himself, and as he advanced cautiously, feeling the furniture gingerly, with fingers outstretched below the level of his waist, he dabbed with his left hand and a large silk handkerchief at his cheek and chin.  He was very neatly dressed; upon his fingers were several heavy encrusted rings; his sockless feet slipped tentatively along the parquet in carpet slippers of blue and white check.  He found a chair beside me; his son, after hovering protectively for a few minutes, withdrew from the room; Joyce remained there, his ringed fingers twitching at the arm of his guilt chair.  From time to time his hand would finger and adjust the loose lenses in his heavy steel spectacles.  His half-blindness was so oppressive that one had the impression of speaking to someone who was very ill indeed.

He appeared to be under the impression that I could do something over in London to induce the Home Secretary to remove the ban upon *Ulysses*.  He spoke gently, in his lovely Livia Plurabelle voice—telling me of the difficulties and injustices he had encountered, telling me of the measures which had been taken to enable his great work to be sold in the United States.  He pronounced the word "Ulysses" in a soft Triestine manner, calling it "Oulissays."  He had formed a plan.  The plan was to send me by registered post from Paris a copy of the de luxe edition of *Ulysses* which would then be confiscated by His Majesty's Customs and Excise.  I should then bring proceedings against the Treasury for having unlawfully detained my property; the case would attract wide

publicity; and the book would be released.  He unfolded this
plan with such innocence and passion that I became embarrassed.  I suggested to him that, were I to bring such an action
against the administration, the Treasury Counsel would assuredly read out to the Court long passages from Mrs. Bloom's
interior monologue and that there were words, phrases and
even paragraphs in that famous reflection which might well
alienate the sympathies of any English court of law.  He said
that he thought I was mistaken.  Only recently the *Sunday
Dispatch* had actually mentioned the book with approval;
surely this meant that the tide of puritan prejudice had
changed?  Moreover the book had recently been blessed by
the Pope.  "By the Pope?" I asked him in astonishment.
"Yes," he answered, "and in St. Peter's itself.  A friend of
mine brought the book with him into the basilica; he knelt as
the Pope passed; he and the book together received the papal
blessing."  As he told me this story the lightest twitch of
amusement passed over his face, brushing his cheek as lightly
as a dragon fly upon a pool.  Again I felt that sense of awe
which only the very sensitive or the very delicate can give.  I
promised to do all I could, and indeed the authorities in London were not, somewhat to my surprise, so unsympathetic.  But
so distressed was I by my own incapacity and toughness, by
the actual delicacy of Joyce's manner and sensibility, that I rose
and left the flat in some embarrassment, making vague promises to his trusting sightless eyes.

It was only when I found myself again outside the door,
smelling again the familiar turpentine smell of all French stair-
cases, that I remembered that I had forgotten to ask James
Joyce about Hamilton Rowan and the Ha Ha.

I might have remained for ever in ignorance of the legend
of Clongowes Wood College had not my friend Mr. Furlong,
Director of the Dublin Art Gallery and himself an old-Clon-
gownian, promised to run the legend to earth.  He discovered
in an old file of the school magazine, dating from 1896, the

very version of the story which must first have come to Joyce's romantic eyes. It runs as follows:

"It is said that a party of soldiers were sent to Rathcoffey to arrest Hamilton Rowan as a United Irishman and the story of his escape from them has been often told. While the soldiers were ascending the stairs, he jumped from the balcony to the lawn below, and, springing on the back of a horse which was grazing hard by, rode straight for Clongowes. His pursuers just reached the hall door at Clongowes in time to see him pass into the 'round room' and immediately fired at him. But he had time to close the door against the slugs, the marks of which can still be seen. We can well imagine with what feelings he entered the room in later years, and with what gratitude he looked on the door that shielded him from the deadly volley.

"From the 'round room' he rushed into the Library, and seeing that one of the windows was open, with wonderful presence of mind, flung out his hat and hid himself in a secret chamber that escaped the notice of his pursuers. They, noting the open window, and the hat lying derelict on the Ha Ha, concluded that he again had risked a dangerous jump, and was still in the open country. Down they sprang in hot pursuit and proceeded to scour the country for their quarry, who meanwhile was well treated by Squire Browne, and baffled every effort to capture him."

Now this incident, if it occurred at all, must have occurred during the fifty anxious hours which Hamilton Rowan spent under the roof of Mr. and Mrs. Sweetman at "Rosedale." Rathcoffey is some thirty miles by road from Baldoyle and the whole countryside was being searched for the escaped prisoner. Hamilton Rowan was well known throughout County Kildare and his enormous bulk (for by then he had become as stout as he was tall) could never have been easy to disguise. I do not seriously believe that even Hamilton Rowan would during those dangerous hours have risked a return to his home. I record the story, since the legend is persistent and must have some foundation. But I do not believe it to be true.

# X

## REIGN OF TERROR, 1794

Lands at Roscoff–Taken to Morlaix–Imprisonment at Brest–His release and interview with Robespierre–Severe illness–The guillotine–A secret report–The 9th Thermidor–The anti-Jacobin reaction–Disgust with French politics–Leaves for America–His foolish journey down the Seine–Mary Wollstonecraft–The *Columbus*.

### ( 1 )

THE SHERIDAN brothers had advised Hamilton Rowan to make for the little port of Roscoff, near Morlaix, upon the coast of Finisterre. It was this small harbour which had witnessed the landing of Mary Stuart when at the age of six she had come to be affianced to the Dauphin of France. It was at Roscoff that the Young Pretender had disembarked after his escape from Scotland in 1746. The place was well known to the Sheridan brothers since it had for many years been a centre of the brandy trade. In more recent times it has specialized in the despatch of early vegetables for the English market.

On entering the bay of Roscoff their little boat was fired on by one of the batteries mounted upon the coast. Hamilton Rowan borrowed a scarlet night-cap belonging to one of the sailors, stuffed it with straw, tied it to a boat-hook and hoisted it, as a cap of liberty, to the mast. Under this symbol they sailed into the harbour and brought up under the old fortress of St. Paul de Léon. Hamilton Rowan handed half the cash in his possession to the Sheridan brothers and to Murphy, climbed on to a neighbouring fishing-boat, and urged his rescuers to make all speed back to Dublin Bay. He himself landed at Roscoff expecting to be welcomed as a friend of the Revolution and an Irish patriot. He was soon disillusioned.

He was escorted to the Hôtel de Ville and interrogated in the court-room by the local commune. He informed them that he had escaped from an English prison in Dublin and showed them a copy of the Dublin *Evening Post* in which had been printed in full the proclamation offering a reward for his arrest. The local commune were not impressed. The chairman, who was also commandant of the fortress, informed him bluntly that as on his own showing he had escaped from prison in Ireland great care would be taken that he should not escape from prison in France. He was therefore confined in a garret in the Hôtel de Ville and a sentry was placed at his door.

At midnight the mayor of Roscoff arrived for a second interview. "He interrogated me," writes Hamilton Rowan, "with more consistency and ingenuity than I had as yet found among my new acquaintance. In the course of my examination his eye turned towards my hat, in which some person in the court-house had put a national cockade; he now rose and tore it out, exclaiming, as if in a violent rage, against me whom he knew to be an English spy, for having thus dared to profane the emblem of liberty." Hamilton Rowan mollified the mayor by asking him to forward a letter to the Committee of Public Safety to whom, he asserted rightly, he was well known. The mayor replied that Jeanbon St. André, a member of the Committee, was at that moment at Brest inspecting the French fleet. Hamilton Rowan therefore asked the mayor to forward a letter direct to St. André. He was then permitted to lie down upon some straw in the corner. Thus passed his first night in Revolutionary France.

On waking next morning he went to his garret window and looked down upon the little harbour below. He was "much mortified" to see Mr. Sweetman's pleasure boat moored among the fishing smacks. When his jailer brought him his breakfast he asked what had happened to the Sheridan brothers and to Murphy. The jailer could give him no information. All he could say was that the boat had been pursued and captured and there it was. Throughout that day Hamilton Rowan paced his little garret in anxiety and distress. In the evening a letter arrived from Jeanbon St. André. He was to be sent to Brest "under a guard of honour." The next morning the guard arrived. It consisted of a Lieutenant Gayson and two other officers who placed Hamilton Rowan in a "sorry equipage" drawn by a "rascally nag." They reached Morlaix in the evening and were lodged in a convent which was being used as a guard-house. The captain of the Guard at Morlaix was a young man of "very prepossessing countenance and pleasing manners." Hamilton Rowan confided to him his distress at his present situation and his anxiety regarding the fate of his family in Ireland. The young man was sympathetic. He also had lost a loving father who had died "not by natural means"; he was obliged to wear the revolutionary uniform in order to protect the remaining members of his family. Here evidently was a gentleman of a type wholly different from that of Lieutenant Gayson and his two companions. On the way from Roscoff these officers had regaled their prisoner by stories of the treatment accorded by them to those of the Vendée rebels who had fallen into their hands. Hamilton Rowan had been shocked by these confessions "which seemed to me," he records, "most atrocious."

Among the papers in the French National Archives which were discovered by my cousin Hans Rowan Hamilton is a report addressed to the Committee of Public Safety by the National Agent of the district of Morlaix. In this he states that an Irishman of the name of Hamilton Rowan had arrived in a small boat at Roscoff; that he had been brought to Morlaix under the escort of Lieutenant Gayson of the Third Battalion of Morbihan; that he had signed a paper asserting that he was "a supporter of the present Government of France and that, wishing to see his own country enjoy the same liberties as France, he had set foot upon French soil." He had upon

examination admitted that he had escaped from the prison of
Newgate in Dublin but had claimed that he was well known
to several members of the Committee of Public Safety who
would assuredly wish to confer with him immediately. Meanwhile he had pleaded earnestly for the release of the three
sailors who, at great risk to themselves, had brought him from
Ireland and who were now under arrest.

On the following morning Hamilton Rowan was replaced in
his "sorry equipage" and continued his journey under the escort
of the blood-thirsty Gayson. They reached Brest late in the
evening and went straight to the lodgings of Jeanbon St. André
only to find that he had gone on board the flagship and that the
fleet was about to sail. Lieutenant Gayson, being anxious to
leave Brest before the city gates were closed, asked Hamilton
Rowan whether he would mind spending the night at the Military Hospital. "I saw," he records, "the delicacy of their situation and answered that I would go wherever they chose."
They therefore took him to the Hôpital des Invalides where
they handed him over to the concierge and took their leave.

It was only after they had gone that he realized that Lieutenant Gayson had in fact dumped him in a prison hospital
and had omitted to explain to the jailer that he was not a captured prisoner but a foreigner of distinction being escorted by
a guard of honour under the instructions of St. André. The
latter by that time was well out to sea, rolling in the great
flagship off Ushant, rolling on towards the glorious first of
June. The prison door clanged behind Hamilton Rowan as
his escort cantered through the streets of Brest hurrying back
to Morlaix before the town gates were closed. His name was
entered in the prison register; he was given a pewter por-
ringer and cup; he was shown the "pressbed" on which he
was expected to lie. The warders in the prison were galley
slaves, whose station in life was designated by a thin wire round
the left ankle. Hamilton Rowan realized to his dismay that
he was regarded by the warders and by his fellow prisoners
as a captured English spy. As the days passed he came to

see that what had at first appeared a provoking but rather comic experience was in fact a situation of great danger. The jailer paid no attention whatsoever to his remonstrances; the letters which he addressed continuously to the Committee of Public Safety went no further than the jailer's office; he found himself caught in a trap from which there seemed to be no escape. From the windows of his prison he could see down into the courtyard below. The building opposite housed the Revolutionary Tribunal, and every afternoon the condemned prisoners were crowded into carts, their arms pinioned behind them, their hair cut short for the guillotine. As viewed from a prison window, the infallibility of the sovereign people, which at Killyleagh or Rathcoffey had seemed so right and simple, assumed more complicated shapes. He was much alarmed.

His release after four weeks of grave anxiety was due, not to any efficiency or care on the part of the revolutionary authorities, but to a pure coincidence.

## (2)

A Mr. Sullivan, an Irishman in the French service, had been appointed by the Committee of Public Safety inspector of prisoners of war. In the course of his duties he visited the Hospital at Brest and happened to be in the jailer's room when one of Hamilton Rowan's by now frantic letters to the Committee was handed in. The jailer threw the letter across to Sullivan. "For goodness' sake," he said, "rid me of this fellow; he is beginning to get upon my nerves; let him either be sent to the guillotine or be sent away." Sullivan read the letter and recognized the name. He identified Hamilton Rowan and at once wrote off to the Committee of Public Safety for instructions. They arrived by return of post. Sullivan was to bring Hamilton Rowan to Paris without a moment's delay. Similar orders had in fact been sent a month before to Roscoff but the mayor had done nothing about them, supposing that by then Hamilton Rowan had already established contact with St. André at Brest.

The next morning Hamilton Rowan left Brest in triumph in the company of Sullivan. They had been provided with a carriage and four horses; a huge tricolor flag fluttered from the roof of the carriage indicating that they were travelling on business of the State. They reached Orléans on the night of June 7. Early the next morning, June 8, 1794, they witnessed the local celebration of the "Feast of the Supreme Being" which the Convention, under the impulse of Robespierre's mysticism, had decreed a month before. Hamilton Rowan watched this ceremony with astonishment:

"On our arrival at Orléans," he writes, "the decree acknowledging God and the immortality of the soul, which had just passed the Convention, was about to be promulgated by a great fête. All the public functionaries of every sort, civil and military, were assembled at the chief church which was then opened to the public. About half-way up the very handsome steeple of the church, a large board was placed, on which the words 'Le peuple français reconnoit l'Etre Suprême et l'Immortalité de l'Ame' was blazoned in large gold letters, with a screen before it. At a signal the screen fell, amidst the firing of cannon and musketry, and bands of music playing, while the multitude responded, 'Vive Robespierre!'"

With that cry still ringing in his ears, Hamilton Rowan re-entered the *berline à quatre chevaux* and was carried at full speed to Paris. The tricolor flag flying from the roof of the carriage indicated that they were important personages travelling on urgent business; they rattled unimpeded through octrois and police barriers; their steaming horses were replaced rapidly at road-side posting offices; they covered the seventy miles to the capital within the space of ten hours. The summer of 1794, the sweltering summer of the Reign of Terror, was one of the hottest ever known. That Sunday, the 8th of June, as is recorded, was a day of scorching sunshine. Hamilton Rowan, rocking by the side of Sullivan in the swaying carriage, was conscious of a pulse of excitement, of the fierce heat which beat up from the cobbled highway, of some inner inflammation throbbing in his veins and head. The trees as they flashed past the carriage windows, the rattle of the wheels upon the cobbles, the cries of the postilions, the murmured and increasingly anxious remarks of Sullivan at his side, fused into a nightmare pattern of dizziness. He could eat nothing and the water that he swallowed at every stopping place appeared insufficient to quench his thirst. The sun set, but the carriage swayed on until the lights of Paris swirled among the trees. When they passed the barrier it was evident that Hamilton Rowan was very ill indeed.

But Sullivan had his orders. The Committee had been horrified to learn that this famous Irish patriot, the man who had all but given his life in order to assist them, had on arrival been abandoned and forgotten in a jail at Brest. The treatment which he had suffered at the hands of the Revolution might well have chilled his sympathies, he might well report back to Ireland the incompetence or unfriendliness of the French Government. The instructions were that immediately upon arrival he should be brought into the presence of the dictator himself and receive from the lips of France's ruler the apologies which were his due. Sullivan dared not disobey these instructions. The great dusty carriage drove straight through the heart of Paris and rumbled into the courtyard of the Tuileries. The palace blazed with candles and the windows on the first floor were open upon the steaming night. They were ushered immediately into Robespierre's room.

The dictator also had had a tiring day. In Paris also that Sunday, the 20th Prairial, had been devoted to the Feast of the Supreme Being. The ceremonies, which had been so elaborately prepared by the painter David, had not been successful. The statue of Atheism, when Robespierre had applied to it the torch of Virtue and Enlightenment, had refused to burn; the adjoining statue of Wisdom had been blackened by smoke. During the long procession from the Tuileries gardens to the

Champ de Mars Robespierre had heard, as an undertone to the cries of approbation from the multitudes, the murmured grumbling, the slight sniggers, of the Deputies who walked behind. He had climbed the artificial mound which had been erected upon the Champ de Mars and had made his carefully prepared oration upon the immortality of the soul. The guns thundered; the flags waved; the burning sunshine glistened upon the troops arrayed around him. But behind him, where the Convention stood massed in sullen hostility, there was a grim silence. The day of his apotheosis had proved the beginning of defeat. He had walked back to the Tuileries conscious that he was surrounded by conspiracy, treachery and hate. And then, at midnight, in the high hot room at the Tuileries, they brought him a huge Irishman, his clothes stained by four weeks of prison, his eyes flashing strangely in the candles of the room.

For Hamilton Rowan that should have been his great moment. Here at last he was brought face to face with the Incorruptible, with the living embodiment of Virtue and the General Will. Never had he felt so strongly in him the desire to please. Never in all his life had he felt so desperately, so uncontrollably ill. He gazed with eyes that refused to focus, upon a little man in a neatly powdered wig; upon a little man in a sky-blue frock coat and white knee-breeches; upon a little man with the face of a young cat and the manners of a dancing master; upon a little man who rasped in a staccato voice, his green spectacles tilted up upon his forehead, his forefinger raised incessantly as he spoke. On the table lay a hat decorated with the great ostrich plumes of red and white and blue, and the faded bouquet of cornflowers, poppies and wheat which Robespierre all day had clenched in his hand. The dry little voice spoke to him and the forefinger was upraised. The thousand candles whirled around him. His brain refused to function, he could not understand or answer; he was dismissed. He was taken by Sullivan to the rooms which had been reserved

for him and a doctor was summoned. He remained dangerously ill from jail-fever for six important weeks. He never
saw Robespierre again.

(3)

I am always fascinated by the part played in human destinies
by the element of chance. Had not Lieutenant Gayson been
in such a hurry to leave Brest that night before the gates closed
he would not have deposited my great-great-grandfather in
the prison hospital or would at least have warned the jailer
that this was no ordinary prisoner but a man whom St. André
and the Committee of Public Safety were most anxious to see.
Had Hamilton Rowan not been confined in the noisome laza-
retto of Brest, he would not have contracted jail-fever and
would have been identified with Robespierre during the weeks
when that dictator was at the summit of his power. And had
he in fact been in close association with the Jacobins between
May and July of 1794 it is much to be doubted whether he
would have escaped the reaction which followed the 9th Thermidor and his head also might have rolled into the basket of
the Place de la Révolution.

As it was, he remained seriously ill during those vital six
weeks. He had been lodged by orders of the Committee in a
"superb suite of apartments" in the Palais Royal then known
as the "Palais Egalité." Monsieur Colon, surgeon general to
the army, was ordered to attend him; and he was accorded a
grant of 1,000 livres from the national funds. After six weeks
of severe illness he was able to attend the Committee of Public
Safety. He was asked a few perfunctory questions and then
dismissed. They were by then far too concerned with the
crisis in their own affairs to attend to any Irish patriot. He
was able none the less to beg them to intercede on behalf of
Parson Jackson who was at that date still awaiting his trial at
Newgate. It was then that he learnt that they had threatened
through the Russian Ambassador, to shoot General O'Hara if
Jackson were harmed. He told them that he did not feel this

menace would create a very deep impression upon the London Cabinet "since the cases were so dissimilar." He advised them rather to seek to bribe Cokayne. They replied "that this had already been attended to." He had by that time managed to open communications with his wife and from her he received some remittances of money. He wisely decided no longer to live on the charity of the Jacobins and transferred himself from the Palais Royal to his old home in the Petit Hôtel de Choiseul in the Rue de Mousseau. This house, which held for him so many happy memories and where his eldest son had been born, was now rented from the Government by a lock-smith who had once been employed at Versailles. While there he witnessed what he calls "several of the inconveniences of a revolutionary Government" and he mentions requisitions, blackmail and general incompetence. He does not mention the Terror, which during those ghastly weeks between June 12 and July 28, 1794, was raging in all its fury. In Paris alone during these days no less than 1225 victims had been killed by the guillotine. He roamed unhappily through those empty rooms, recognizing familiar pieces of furniture from happier days, distracted by the carnage around him—disillusioned, anxious, depressed. A few of his letters to his wife during these sad months have been preserved. "I am unmanned," he wrote to her, "when I think I have lost your regard; and I am desperate when I reflect that I deserve it."

He makes no mention in his autobiography of any further conversations with the French Government. He assured Wolfe Tone, when he met him later in Philadelphia, that he had handed in "some memorials on the state of Ireland." He had hoped much for success but his hopes were dashed by the fall of Robespierre and his execution on July 28. He did not witness that event, but he was informed that the crowd in their fury "had thrust their umbrellas into the waggon against his body."

Two days later, however, he was present in the Place de la Concorde when the whole Commune of Paris, numbering some sixty persons, were guillotined within the space of an hour and a half. He heard the rumble of the carts; he heard the rattle of the drums; he heard the three dread sounds of execution—the slap of the board as it swung into place, the jangle of the iron clamp which secured the victim, the thud of the knife itself. He did not enjoy the spectacle. "Though I was standing," he wrote, "above a hundred paces from the place of execution, the blood of the victims streamed under my feet." As the heads fell one by one the crowd yelled, "A bas le maximum," referring thereby to Robespierre's perfectly reasonable attempts to prevent a rise in prices. He walked back to the Hôtel de Choiseul, his shoes stained with blood, pondering upon Virtue and the General Will.

That he had hoped much from Robespierre and the Jacobins is evident from a curious paper which the industry of my cousin Hans Rowan Hamilton has unearthed from the French National Archives. The memorandum is undated and unsigned but is evidently the report of some official sent to interview Hamilton Rowan on the prospects of a French invasion of Ireland.

According to this document Hamilton Rowan had stated that the whole population of Ireland "except the Episcopalians" were discontented with English rule, and that the Catholics and the Dissenters would rise if assured of French support. He had added that the Irish had no wish to exchange English tyranny for French protection, that they were frightened of being turned into a French province, and that the invading army should for this reason not be too large and should from the outset issue a proclamation guaranteeing Irish independence. Three quarters of the militia, he assured the French Government, "would leave their flag for the flag of liberty." Moreover two thirds of the English fleet were manned by Irish sailors who "would not fail to fly to the aid of their native country."

In forwarding this report to the Committee of Public Safety the anonymous official adds some comments of his own.

"Given these facts," he writes, "here is the plan which I have conceived." A French army of 30,000 men was to be landed in Ireland in three separate groups, at Kinsale, at Wexford, and in the Bay of Galway. The Irish should be invited to form Convocations to decide their own future form of government. The lands of the gentry and those of Trinity College, Dublin, should be distributed among the peasantry. The Wexford army should march straight on Dublin where it would eventually be joined by the two other armies. The memorandum continues as follows: "Hamilton Rowan, that illustrious martyr to Liberty, should lead the Wexford army; his manifesto would infallibly stir the people of Dublin, whose idol he is; he is moreover the most striking patriot in Ireland; the veneration of the Irish for him is such that if they had the idea of giving themselves a King the majority of votes would combine in favour of Hamilton Rowan. This man is necessary, therefore, to lead that part of the army which should appear first before Dublin; from the little conversation I have had with him he would answer with his head for the rising of nine tenths of the people of Dublin. Added to this his name at the head of the French Army would completely reassure the Irish as to the motives of the invasion which had just taken place among them."

It may well have been that Hamilton Rowan hoped at one moment to be crowned at Tara. These hopes were dashed by the death of Robespierre and the collapse of the Jacobins. "From this period," he writes, "everything bore a new face. Marat's bust and the *bonnet de liberté* were torn down and trampled upon in the theatres and other public places. . . . It now became a measure of personal safety to be able to declare that one had been imprisoned during Robespierre's tyranny. It was dangerous even to appear a Jacobin, as several persons were murdered in the streets by *La Jeunesse Parisienne* merely because they wore long coats and short hair."

He decided to leave the blood and muddle of revolutionary

Paris for the higher and more settled ideals of the American Republic. He describes himself in his autobiography as "being much discontented" with the state of Paris, where they were too busy from their own intestine divisions to think of assisting Ireland, or anything beneficial to others. He therefore applied to Madgett for a passport to the New World.

## (4)

Hamilton Rowan, as we have seen, possessed no sense of the effect of his actions upon others. Although his mind was in no way original, he had an irritating habit of doing things in an unusual way. He knew that the country, in the spring of 1795, was in a disturbed state; he knew that the Paris mob were highly suspicious and intractable; he should have learnt from his experiences at Brest that it was difficult for a man speaking with an English accent to avoid the suspicion of being a spy. Yet instead of taking ordinary precautions in his journey to the coast he chose a means of transport which even in the most normal circumstances a Frenchman would regard as *invraisemblable*. He decided to leave Paris in a Thames wherry.

He had bought the boat at the sale of Philippe Egalité's effects. He said good-bye to the Rue de Mousseau and packed his luggage, his money, his *nécessaire*, or tiring equipage, and his dog Charles into the little skiff and then started off to row to Havre. He bore a false passport in the name of James Thomson, a reputed merchant of South Carolina. He carried with him a letter from James Monroe, at that time Minister American in Paris, to Edmund Randolph, the United States Secretary of State. He also carried a certificate showing that during his residence in Paris he had fulfilled his duty as a national guard. He hoped that these documents would enable him to row to Havre unmolested. They did not.

As his little boat shot under the bridge of Port Royal he was observed by a member of the proletariat who raised the cry that a deputy was escaping with the nation's gold. The man had a musket which he kept on aiming at the wherry, and Hamilton Rowan felt that it would be more prudent to land. As he approached the landing stage by the Porte Chaillot the man with the musket jumped into the river and seized him by the shoulder. In the scuffle which ensued the wherry shipped a fair amount of water and an excited crowd gathered on the bank. Hamilton Rowan demanded to be taken to the guard-room at the Passy octroi. His papers were examined and pro-nounced perfectly in order. This decision satisfied neither the crowd nor the man with the musket. The latter still held him firmly by the collar, while the former started shouting "à la lanterne." He was dragged before the mayor of Passy and his captor, who was intoxicated with liquor and the plaudits of the multitude, explained that nobody but a deputy escaping with the nation's gold would wish to row to Havre in gloves. The mayor complimented the crowd upon their vigilance and patriotism but assured them that their prisoner was not a deputy but a citizen of the United States whose papers were in perfect order. He was allowed to rejoin his boat in which, to his surprise, he found his belongings and his dog Charles still intact. He pushed off and drifted half a mile down the river. Observing a shelving bank where some women were washing clothes he decided to pull in and bail out his wherry which was very wet. The washerwomen, however, started screaming and clapping their hands. Again he was dragged before the mayor of Passy to whom the washerwomen ex-plained that they had caught a deputy escaping with the na-tion's gold. The mayor complimented them upon their vig-ilance and patriotism and for the second time examined Ham-ilton Rowan's papers. He was then allowed to push off again, and floated down the river keeping to midstream. He reached Rouen in four days. "My mode of travelling," he comments, "was certainly novel, and created more suspicion during the whole route than I had been aware of." At Rouen he remained three days, and thereafter abandoned his boat and took the diligence to Havre.

While in Paris he had made the acquaintance of Mary Wollstonecraft, author of *The Vindication of the Rights of Women* and mother of Mary Shelley. Miss Wollstonecraft had contracted a "republican" marriage with an American of the name of Gilbert Imlay and was at the time living in a cottage outside Paris. "My society," writes Hamilton Rowan, "which before this time was entirely male, was now most agreeably increased and I got a dish of tea and an hour's rational conversation whenever I called on her. . . . Her manners were interesting, and her conversation spirited, yet not out of the sex!" They became warm friends, and during the few days he was at Havre waiting for a boat to take him to America he stayed, in spite of the owner's absence, in a house owned by Imlay, in the town. There was only one boat in the harbour sailing for the United States, the *Columbus*, Captain John Dillon of Baltimore. When he first applied for a passage, under his assumed name of Thomson, the captain said that his cabin was engaged and that there was no other berth available. Hamilton Rowan then decided to reveal his real name, on hearing which Captain Dillon was much impressed, offered to find him accommodation and even altered his bills of lading so as to show that among his passengers was Mr. James Thomson of South Carolina, an American merchant returning with his property. Four days later they set sail for the Asylum of Liberty.

# XI

## AMERICAN EXILE, 1795-1800

Reaches Philadelphia–Joined by Wolfe Tone–The latter leaves
for France and Napper Tandy follows him–The Bantry Bay ex-
pedition–Arrest and death of Tone–Hamilton Rowan leaves Phila-
delphia for Wilmington–His views on American life–His poverty
–Starts business as a calico printer–He fails–Brews and sells beer–
His friends at Wilmington–Refuses to sue for pardon–Mrs.
Rowan and Lord Clare–He is allowed to return to Europe–
Journey to Hamburg–Reunited with his family.

### (1)

THE *Columbus* was a sound but slow-moving ship—"this lump
of a *Columbus*" he called her—and the time hung heavy on
his hands. When they were two days out from Havre they
were hailed by a British frigate, the *Melampus*. An officer
came on board, examined the ship's papers and cross-questioned
the passengers. "Your name is Thomson, Sir," he said to
Hamilton Rowan. "I understand this cargo belongs to you."
"Only a part," answered Rowan. He was quite prepared, if
necessary, to answer questions about South Carolina and
Charleston; the memory of those care-free days when as an
undergraduate he had accompanied Lord Charles Montagu to
that disgruntled colony were lucid in his mind. The *Columbus* meanwhile had swung round until she was close under the
stern of the British frigate; Hamilton Rowan was still talking
to the officer upon the quarter deck when looking up he saw
the name *Melampus* scrolled around the carved windows of the
stern cabin. He asked the officer the name of his captain. On
hearing the name of Sir John Borlase Warren, with whom as

an undergraduate he had skated so gaily upon the Dutch canals, Mr. James Thomson of Charleston found it necessary to retire below decks.

Apart from this; apart from their meeting a derelict upon the high seas; apart from their constant anxiety regarding Barbary or Bermuda pirates; apart from the petty squabbles among the other passengers; the voyage was uneventful and long. Hamilton Rowan found the cabin too congested and the company uncongenial. He moved into the steerage, in which he rigged up a little cubicle for himself. "In here," he wrote to his wife, "I have my cot slung in the middle; my dejuné [*sic*], writing box and trunk, on the one side; in the other my two camp chairs and a little writing table, where I am now seated writing to my love." The more obtrusive of his fellow passengers did not respect his solitude; he screened his cubicle from the rest of the ship by stretching a Union Jack between two marling spikes; upon this he hung a notice "*Respectez les propriétés*" and was thereafter undisturbed.

During those June and July days when the *Columbus* wallowed heavily in great seas and contrary winds, he had many hours in which to contemplate the errors of the past and the chill prospects of the future. For an ideal of liberty he had sacrificed his wife, his children, his fortune, his reputation and his freedom. There he remained, a solitary ageing outlaw, alone save for his dog Charles and his portmanteau, in the hold of a reeling reeking ship. These were stern and squalid realities; but was the ideal for which he had made these harsh surrenders in itself a reality? How young, how invigorating and how true had seemed the formulas of revolution when murmured to oneself in the warm library at Rathcoffey or upon the wind-swept ramparts of Killyleagh! The timbers of the old ship groaned above him; at each lurch and movement he felt a stab of rheumatism in his bones; he ached, as he sat there, with home-sickness, disillusion and remorse.

"I sometimes fret," he wrote to his wife on June 28, "and

am grown thin; the clothes you saw me in are now fully large enough; I keep them as a memento. . . . As soon as I arrive in America I shall make up a little package of presents. I fear I shall not be able to muster articles for every one of our little pugs. I have a gold pen and pencil, however, for William; I have a very fine mother-of-pearl and paper lanthern for whichever of the ladies is mamma's messenger; and this, I shrewdly believe is Harriet, if she be not too fat. I have a little dejuné for the corrector of my press, Jane. I have a gold-bladed and agate-handled powder-knife for mamma; and a silver watch chain which William may give to Thom if he pleases. In short I have very little; but what little I have, or ever shall have, will be never so well used, or so pleasurably destined by me, as to you and them. It is thus I sometimes amuse myself; at other times I curse my cruelty and harshness to you and them; and with the most sincere sorrow I recollect that the last time William came to me to say his lesson, I gave way to my own agitated state of mind, and sent him away in anger. But of what avail now to recollect all the little and the great injustices of which I have been guilty. God bless you all! Good night!"

As he thought of these small and happy things there echoed in his ears the voices and laughter of the children whom he might never see again. But there were other echoes that rumbled in the passages of his brain. The sound of heavy locks turning at Newgate; the sound of the tumbrils in the courtyard at Brest; the rattle and thud of the guillotine; the mob screaming "à la lanterne"; the crowd shouting at Orléans "Vive Robespierre"; the crowd, but a few weeks later yelling "A bas le maximum" as the blood seeped slowly among the cobblestones of the Place de la Révolution; the washerwomen at Passy clapping wet hands.

"I own to you candidly," he wrote to his wife, "when it is of no avail, that my ideas of reform, and of another word which begins with the same letter, are very much altered by living for twelve months in France; and that I never wish to see

HAMILTON ROWAN AS AN OLD MAN

*See page 158*

THE CASTLE GATE-HOUSE AND THE TOWN OF KILLYLEAGH

See page 194

either the one or the other procured by force. I have seen one faction rising over another and overturning it; each of them in their turn making a stalking-horse of the supreme power of the people, to cover public and private massacre and plunder; while every man of virtue and humanity shuddered and skulked in a disgraceful silence. . . . You know there were some lengths to which I never went; and I am sorry to find your opinion of one who did, so bad."

The *Columbus* anchored at Philadelphia on July 17, 1795.

(2)

The person referred to in the last sentence of the above letter was of course, Theobald Wolfe Tone. Mrs. Hamilton Rowan attributed all the disasters which had overwhelmed her husband and her family to the sinister influence of this remarkable man. "As to that wretch Tone," she had written, "God forbid that I should have any intercourse with one who, by his wicked principles and artifice, has ruined those most dear to me." "All your faults," she wrote again, "originated with your connecting yourself with wicked and artful men who cared not for you or for anybody else. And now for mercy's sake give up the idea of reforming the State in any way, however peaceable it may be."

Her anxiety and hatred were increased when, in June 1795, she heard that Tone, in virtue of his "compromise" with the Government, had sailed with his wife and children for America. "The arch-deceiver Tone," she wrote to her husband, "has quit the country and it is feared he may go where you are. I think it my duty to say that, if this should be the case, you ought to avoid all connection with him. It is as well to say at once what is the fact: *his friend cannot be mine;* his wicked principles and artful manners have destroyed us."

I must admit that my great-great-grandmother had some cause to be annoyed. She was a strong-minded woman and it was her loyalty and persistence that in the end secured her husband's pardon. I have nothing but admiration for her courage and good sense. But her excellent qualities as wife and mother were marred by a streak of meanness which chills my sympathy. She behaved meanly to Mrs. Sweetman about payment for the boat; she behaved meanly, in spite of the desperate appeals made to her by her husband, to the Sheridan brothers and to Murphy. And the reproaches which, with some excuse, she addressed to him in America were on occasions so subtly contrived as to indicate a streak of cruelty. On arrival at Philadelphia, for instance, he found waiting for him a parcel of books and clothing, including a miniature of herself, on the back of which was encased a lock of hair. Observing that there were some white hairs in the locket he assumed she had mingled his father's locks with her own. He thanked her for this graceful thought. She replied with asperity. "You mistake as to any of the hair being your father's. For well as I know your affection for him, I should not think of putting his and mine together. A few days after we parted several hairs, whiter than age can make them, appeared on my forehead; this no doubt was occasioned by sorrow, for it soon ceased; my maid pulled them out and there was enough to make a small plait." One cannot regard this as the letter of an agreeable woman.

Her immediate apprehensions were, none the less, fully justified. Tone and his family arrived in Philadelphia in August 1795 and established themselves in the boarding house where Hamilton Rowan and Napper Tandy were also staying. Before leaving Dublin Tone had had a final meeting with Russell and Emmet in the latter's "elliptical study" at Rathfarnham, and had pledged himself to obtain French assistance for the liberation of Ireland. Before leaving Belfast he had repeated this vow upon the top of Cave Hill in the company of Russell, Samuel Neilson and McCracken. He informed Hamilton Rowan of his intentions and the latter offered to introduce him to Citizen Anet, the French Minister to the United States. Tone replied that there were many English agents in

Philadelphia, that Hamilton Rowan's movements were certainly being watched, and that he would prefer to visit Citizen Anet alone. The French Minister was not encouraging and Tone retired to Princeton where he bought an estate of 180 acres for the sum of £1180 and decided to establish himself as an American farmer. His active, heroic nature chafed under these prosperous and sedentary conditions. He did not appreciate the virtues of the Americans. He found them "a selfish, churlish, unsocial race, totally absorbed in making money." "The spirit of commerce," he wrote, "hath eaten up all their feeling." At that moment in November 1795 he received letters from Keogh and Russell in Ireland assuring him that the people were "rapidly advancing towards republicanism" and that the moment for action was at hand. He again visited Citizen Anet at Philadelphia whom on this occasion he found full of encouragement and readiness to assist. Bidding farewell to his family he sailed from Sandy Hook on January 1, 1796. Hamilton Rowan remained in Philadelphia; he had had more than enough of France.

The consequences of Tone's fateful journey are known to history. By the sheer force of his conviction, he managed to convert Carnot and Hoche to his ideas. The failure of the Bantry Bay expedition of 1796 as of the Texel expedition of 1797 discouraged the Directory but encouraged the Irish patriots. In December 1797 Tone had an interview with General Bonaparte in his house in the Rue Chantereine. The General in a "low and hollow" voice discussed the possibility of a third expedition to synchronize with a rising of the Irish peasantry. The rebellion of 1798 was the result. General Humbert landed at Castlebar but was forced to surrender before he reached Dublin. The *Anacreon*, packed with United Irishmen including Napper Tandy, having reached the Isle of Arran, turned tail and fled to Norway. The third French expedition entered Lough Swilly where on October 12 they were attacked by a British Fleet under the command of Sir John Borlase Warren. Tone, who had accompanied this expedition in the

*Hoche*, was one of the first prisoners to step on shore. He was immediately recognized and arrested. On reaching Dublin he preferred suicide to the ignominy of the gallows. He slit his throat with a penknife and after lingering for a week in agony died on November 19, 1798. He was buried in his grandfather's grave at Bodenstown.

(3)

I had always imagined that my great-great-grandfather had become disgusted with Irish politics when he realized that his former associates in the Society of United Irishmen had been directly responsible for the horrors of the 1798 rebellion and for the invasion of their country by foreign armies. On examining his papers more closely I find that his change of heart began in December 1795 immediately prior to Tone's departure for Europe. They had sat up late that night at Princeton, indulging, as Tone records "in that kind of animated and enthusiastic conversation which our characters and the nature of the enterprise I was embarked in may be supposed to give rise to." Hamilton Rowan returned from Princeton to the boarding house at Philadelphia and to the society of a drunken Napper Tandy. He was sick to death of enthusiastic or bibulous conversation, nor did he feel that Ireland would really benefit by an invasion of the sansculottes. He had come to doubt even his own suitability for political life. He decided to leave Philadelphia, where he was the object of attention from British agents who asked him "inquisitive questions." He decided no further to "agitate politics" a pursuit to which he now found himself unfitted and which, he confesses to his wife, "would make you think not only meanly of my sense but also lightly of my life."

"Finding," he records in his memoirs, "the violence of party in Philadelphia and what appeared to me the imprudent interference of some of my countrymen in their politics which it was almost impossible to avoid I rejoiced in my determination of quitting that great and flourishing town."

He toyed for a time with the idea of buying land in one of the "unsettled" areas and establishing himself as a farmer. "I will go to the woods," he wrote to his wife, "but I will not kill Indians or keep slaves. Good God! If you heard some of the Georgians or Kentucky people talk of killing the natives! Cortes and all that followed him were not more sanguinary in the South than they would be in North America."

His first impressions of America had been most favourable. "I have met," he wrote from Philadelphia, "with more than civilities; I have met with a degree of friendship here which I could not have conceived." This impression was not permanent. "I do not," he wrote six months later, "promise to remain here. Indeed I cannot—disgusted as I am by the rough manners of the people; the great expense of procuring those mental gratifications which are so superior to eating and drinking; the universal rage of money getting; and the decided separation of parties. But what can I do? I must be mad indeed if I entertained any hope of returning to Ireland." He was shocked to observe how quickly the Americans, having united to obtain their independence, had relapsed into partisanship. "Of party," he writes, "there is much, as violent and more gross than ever I saw in Europe. As to education, it is very superficial and I think very much neglected. The liberty granted to children of both sexes is much greater than we can conceive, and very licentious indeed were the generality of youth that I have seen. When you get into the country parts you see a different race of people—you meet with many who remind you of what John Bull once was—frank, open, hospitable and independent; but near the coast you have the spawn of the refuse of England, and among the borderers the refuse of Ireland; they have the same character with respect to Englishmen that Portuguese are said to have in respect to Spaniards. Speculation is the soul of the American."

How lovely, how auspicious, how awe-inspiring had seemed to him, but a year ago, the Declaration of Independence! "We hold these truths to be self-evident"—the phrase had echoed through his brain as the exordium to some majestic incantation. "That all men are created equal"—here again were words which stirred the very fibres of his heart. For this, as for those other fictions of the General Will and Sovereign People, he had risked his life and happiness. The blood had spread slowly in and out of the cobble-stones of the Place de la Révolution. And even here, in the new free world, there was dissension and materialism. Even in divine America the rights of man were not self-evident. The Africans were not regarded as equal;—they were sold as slaves; the Indians were not regarded as equal;—they were massacred in droves. In France, in the United States, the tyrants and the oligarchs had been destroyed by force; but human nature, —envious and greedy, corruptible and cruel—had reasserted her sway.

Clearly, during these months he was learning something from reality. His wife, having received the letter in which he confessed that he was disillusioned by the French revolution, had replied in what he called "a scolding letter." "It is with the highest satisfaction," she had written meanly, "that I learn that your residence in France has so altered your opinions on political subjects. It would have been well, most certainly, if this happy chance had been brought about at a less price than it has cost you. . . . You do not use your own understanding sufficiently, from some error in your education or temper, but catch your opinions and ideas from those immediately about you. I am doubtful whether nature ever did intend you for a public character."

To which he humbly replied:—"The fact is that from education and principle I was led to assert, and attempt to support, a reform of parliament and equal liberty to all religious sects.

Association may have, and certainly did, lead me more into active life than I wished, was fit for, or will ever (in any case on this side of eternity) fall into again."

In such a mood he decided to leave Philadelphia, the atmosphere of which was too "political"; he retired to the little town of Wilmington on the banks of the Delaware.

## (4)

Hamilton Rowan was at that date forty-five years of age; he had still thirty-eight years of life before him. Of his eleven years of exile, five were passed in America, four of them being spent in or near Wilmington. After his escape a sentence of outlawry had been passed upon him on the ground that he did "cause, procure and incite persons exercising the power of government in France, being enemies of our said Lord the King, to invade his Kingdom of Ireland with ships and armed men." Under this sentence his life and property were forfeited to the crown. The financial affairs of Hamilton Rowan are wrapped in perpetual mystery but of his income at the time of his escape there is no doubt at all; it amounted exactly to £8,121 12s. 9d. a year. In theory the Government were entitled to confiscate the whole of this large fortune. The Chancellor, Lord Clare, had, however, always regarded Hamilton Rowan with amused if irritated respect; according to Charles Phillipps, he held the view that Rowan had been "trepanned" at the time of the Jackson episode and had been more sinned against than sinning. He therefore allowed Mrs. Hamilton Rowan to collect such rents as she could extract from the tenants. Since she was unable to proceed against them at law, and since they were themselves aware of this disability, the sums she extracted were few and far between. They enabled her, however, to educate her children and even, from time to time, to send small sums to her husband in America. It is evident, however, that during those four years at Wilmington he lived in circumstances of penury and distress.

Such references to his American exile as he included in his Autobiography are colourless and sparse. Mr. A. Hamilton Rowan of New York City has, however, been so kind as to help me in obtaining further particulars regarding the sad sojourn of our common ancestor at Wilmington. The Historical Society of Delaware have given us that generous and efficient assistance which is characteristic of all branches of United States Scholarship. From these sources I have been able to add some pathetic details to the reticent account which he wrote himself.

On reaching Wilmington from Philadelphia, he lodged for some months at the house of Mr. Armor, in whose garden he worked for wages as a day labourer. He then took a room in the suburbs of the town, over a back building attached to the house of an eccentric old bachelor. The latter appears to have imagined that Hamilton Rowan was determined to commit suicide and would burst in upon his solitude at all hours of the day and night. During these months the exile maintained himself by brewing spruce or birch beer which he delivered in person to the citizens of the town. Rumours of this employment reached the ears of Mrs. Hamilton Rowan, who protested against such degradation. "In abject dependence," he replied, "I will not live while I can clean boots in an alley." He made friends in Wilmington—the Dickinson family, Caesar Rodney, Mr. Bayard, Dr. Tilton and the Quaker Poole. These were simple people, almost as poor as he was himself; he enjoyed their company and retained their friendship. For the more prosperous Americans he had little sympathy. "O upstart aristocracy," he wrote, "what a fiend art thou!"

His experiences in Wilmington had a sobering effect. When in later years he obtained his pardon and his property he attached to the door of one of the turret rooms at Killyleagh a large label bearing the word "Wilmington." And when, as often happened, the old fires of recklessness or pugnacity began to crackle, he would retire to this reminiscent room and regain his calm.

When money at last arrived from home he left the town of Wilmington and built for himself "a cottage of rough boards" in a meadow opposite the Old Barley Mill on Brandywine creek. According to Elizabeth Montgomery's *Reminiscences of Wilmington* this cabin contained several rooms "each having a fine name." In March 1797 he started a business for the printing of calico. "You will find," he wrote to his wife, "that I am no longer a gentleman, but a printer and dyer of calicoes." The same idea was expressed by him in the circular which he issued to prospective customers:

"It was once Hamilton Rowan, Esq.
Now it is calico printer and dyer."

The business failed and in a few months he inserted the following frank advertisement in the *Delaware Gazette:* "Any person inclining to sacrifice his property by carrying on this manufactury in America may have the whole for one half of the sum they cost." Some pathetic remnants of his experiments in calico printing still exist. But in the end his cabin on the creek caught fire and he lost most of his possessions. He faced these disasters with humorous calm.

It has been recorded by those who remember him at this time that he sought to relieve the tedium of his exile and the gnawings of remorse by indulging in violent physical exercise. "He was famous," writes a Mr. Frank Romer, "for his endurance hikes. Setting out on rainy mornings Mr. Rowan would lie prone in the first pool to soak himself before the downpour wetted him." Mrs. Montgomery in her *Reminiscences of Wilmington* records vividly enough how he and some of his neighbours would indulge in "a Scotch game called curling." "They drew," she writes, "a circle in the ice, and had a stone round but rather flat on one side, in size and shape much like an old-fashioned roll of tobacco; in this a handle was placed, by which it was pushed over the ice, something like pitching quoits. This game has long been forgotten like those who took delight in it."

Meanwhile his wife in Ireland was working persistently to obtain some alleviation of his condition. He had written a letter to an old family friend, Mr. Richard Griffith, expressing contrition for past errors and a firm determination never again to become involved in politics. Mr. Griffith showed this letter to Lord Clare, who dropped a hint that if Hamilton Rowan could be induced to repeat such sentiments in a petition addressed to King George something might well be done. Delighted by this assurance Mr. Griffith informed Mrs. Hamilton Rowan and even drafted with his own hand the form of petition which he felt her husband ought to sign. The text of this most tactless draft was as follows:

"Misguided by false lights and hurried away by presumptuous self-sufficiency, your petitioner dared for a moment to entertain the wild idea of endeavouring, by the aid of Your Majesty's enemies, to reform what he deemed to be the grievances of his native country. But by the intervention of Divine Providence the scheme of destruction was frustrated, and your petitioner, abashed and confounded, fled from the justice of that country. . . . Disgusted by the scenes of carnage which hourly occupied the public attention during his stay in Paris, your petitioner at length obtained permission (after repeated entreaty) to leave a country doomed to misery by the same presumptuous confidence in false philosophy which had misguided your petitioner. Your petitioner, having proceeded to America, and having had full time to reflect upon the folly and turpitude of his conduct, is strongly impressed with the desire of making the only atonement in his power by a public confession of his guilt.

"He therefore humbly implores Your Majesty graciously to accept the deep contrition of a heart truly penitent for past errors and fraught with the warmest attachment to the British constitution and to Your Majesty's person and government."

Hamilton Rowan, as might have been foreseen, was much incensed by being asked to sign so humiliating a version of his

own character and conduct.   His reply to Mr. Griffith is dignified and to the point.   "I never will," he wrote, "sign a petition or declaration in favour of the British constitution in Ireland, which embraces such flagrant abuses as I have witnessed
and of which I have been in some measure the victim.   I would
have promised a perfect quiescence under the present Government and should have been sincerely grateful to those who had
it in their power to crush my family through me, yet forebore.
But my opinions were not hastily adopted; they were neither
the result of pride, of ambition, nor of vanity; they were the
result of the most mature reflection of which I was capable;
they cannot alter, and although I might desist from acting upon
them, I never will disown them."

Mrs. Rowan, on receiving this letter, detected in it that note
of obstinacy which she alone knew how to circumvent.   She
abandoned all hope of an immediate pardon and concentrated
her energy on obtaining permission for her husband to reside
in some neutral European country where she could join him.
She was at pains to deny rumours that had circulated in Dublin to the effect that Hamilton Rowan had been on board the
French fleet at the time of Bantry Bay; she was assiduous in
convincing Lord Clare that, when others of the United Irishmen had taken part in the 1798 rebellion, her husband had
remained quietly at Wilmington, printing his calicoes, selling
his beer, or rowing with his dogs upon the Delaware.   She
was able even to produce a letter from him forecasting the
necessity of an Act of Union, which indeed he welcomed as
implying "the downfall of one of the most corrupt assemblies
as ever, I believe, existed."

Her efforts were successful.   Writing to his sister after the
collapse of the 1798 rising, William Drennan adds a bitter note
on the subject of the Hamilton Rowan family:

"The Chancellor rode up the other day to Mrs. Rowan's carriage, congratulated her on the behaviour of Mr. H. R. for some
time past, so opposite to that of his former political companions,
and assured her that at the conclusion of the war, such conduct

must facilitate his return to his country, his wife and his property. Their son here is a complete convert to maternal opinion and the leniency of Government and is eager to serve in army or navy against the common enemy."

Among the archives at Dublin there is a letter addressed to the Chancellor by Mrs. Hamilton Rowan and dated August 9, 1799, in which she begs that her husband may be allowed to come to Europe. "If," she writes, "I should be so fortunate as to receive a favourable answer, the first wish of my heart will be complied with; and if not, I shall be sensible that there is nothing which can longer delay me in joining my husband in America, where, though I cannot alter the climate, I shall at least enjoy the comfort of alleviating the sufferings of the being most dear to me."

Lord Clare passed this letter on to Mr. Edward Cooke, the Government Secretary, with the following minute:

"I send you a letter from my almost daily oratrix, Mrs. Hamilton Rowan. She is much to be pitied and I cannot see any objection to allowing her husband to quit America with an assurance that if he should be intercepted by a British cruiser on his passage that he should not be brought home and hanged. If you recollect I forwarded her suit for this act of grace some months ago. He has certainly some merit in not being so abandoned as his old colleagues."

"It is too provoking," adds Lord Clare in this minute, "that the old bitch Lord Keith should have let the French and Spanish fleets slip him as they have done. Most probably he will be advanced to the English peerage for this exploit."

Clare's intervention was successful. Four weeks later Mrs. Hamilton Rowan received from Lord Castlereagh, then Chief Secretary, a letter dated September 9, 1799, assuring her that her husband might reside in Europe without molestation "so long as he continues to demean himself in such a manner as not to give offence."

In delighted triumph she conveyed this news to Wilmington.

## (5)

The most irritating feature of my great-great-grandfather's otherwise amiable character was his inability either to foresee the consequence of his conduct or to estimate the impression which it had left upon other people. He was at this stage anxious to redeem his past and to make his peace with the Government. There were many neutral countries in Europe in which he might have settled with his family and confirmed by his innocence the favourable impression which his behaviour in America had created. It was suggested, for instance, that they should take up their residence in Lisbon or Oporto, where he would have found many amenities, an excellent climate, and the eventual prospect of obtaining his pardon. He refused, however, to submit himself to "a petticoat government," referring thereby to the system of the demented Maria I. He preferred Hamburg, the one neutral place in Europe which was calculated again to bring him under suspicion with the English authorities. It was from Hamburg that Napper Tandy had been kidnapped and deported. It was through Hamburg that the Irish revolutionaries were known to maintain their most constant communication with the French Directorate. It was at Hamburg that Pamela Fitzgerald, widow of the unfortunate Lord Edward, was then living at the Matthiessen house on the Speersort, her every action and association being reported to London by Samuel Turner, known to the English Secret Service as "Lord Downshire's friend." Of all the cities of free Europe, Hamburg was the most expensive and the most provocative he could have chosen; the needle of his indiscretion turned to Hamburg with unerring aim.

He sailed from Philadelphia on July 6, 1800, accompanied, as was his habit, by an opossum, his dog, a red bird, and a bag of bird-seed. The opossum escaped into the rigging and was seen no more; the bird sang "so loud and early" that it had to be removed; he was left with his dog Sally, Charles having been drowned in the waters of the Delaware River. He spent his evenings playing "God Save the King" and "Foot's minuet" upon the flute. On August 13 they entered the North Sea; he was almost ill with excitement at the prospect of seeing his family again after five weary years.

Mrs. Hamilton Rowan had already written warning him that he would not find her as young or as amenable as she had been in 1795. "You expect," she had written, "to find me altered, so much as to feel we shall not again be as happy as we were. In person, to be sure, I am altered; perhaps also in manners. When you recollect the scenes I have had to go through, and the courage that was necessary for them, you will naturally suppose that there is more of independence in my character and manners than there was when you left me. This, however, was even then coming fast; I must own, I think, an improvement; prepare yourself to think so, and rest assured my heart and mind are just those you have so long loved."

He was by no means deterred by this warning. The moment his ship berthed at Cuxhaven he sent her a letter of excited anticipation. "My heart beats," he wrote to her, "with as high throbs of affection and anxiety for our expected meeting, as if I were that age when you blessed me with the charms of seventeen."

Mrs. Rowan received this letter "with ecstasy" and made immediate preparations to start for Germany. From Shrewsbury, on her way to London, she told him the date and vessel on which she was sailing. He must come to Cuxhaven to meet her and the little pugs. He would find "a woman whose affection for you is unbounded and who at this instant is scarcely capable of writing, from the agitation occasioned by the prospect of our soon being united."

# XII

## PARDON, 1800–1805

Sir James Crawford and Napper Tandy–Hamilton Rowan settles
at Altona–Financial difficulties–He is allowed to come to England
–Death of his father–The Ursula incident–He crosses to Dublin
and sues for pardon–His outlawry reversed–The return to Killyleagh–End of the United Irishmen–His visits to Dublin–Percy
Bysshe Shelley–Joins Catholic Association–Is attacked in the
House of Commons–Challenges Mr. Dawson to a duel–The Rotunda meeting of 1829–Old age and death.

### (1)

On his arrival at Hamburg, Hamilton Rowan, with his accustomed optimism, called upon the British Resident, Sir James
Crawford, and left with him by means of introduction a copy
of the letter which Lord Castlereagh had sent to Mrs. Rowan.
This letter, it will be remembered, said no more than that
her outlawed husband might come to Europe without fear of
molestation by British frigates on the way. Few British Ministers would have regarded such a letter as implying that Hamilton Rowan should at once be entertained at the British Legation and thereafter officially introduced to Hamburg society.
Sir James Crawford was especially averse from Irish outlaws
since it was he who had created an international incident and
damaged his own diplomatic reputation by kidnapping Napper
Tandy in 1798.

Tandy, who always regarded himself as the sole military
mind in the whole Society of United Irishmen, had been enraged by Tone's success with Citizen Anet. He had left Philadelphia hurriedly and followed Tone to Paris where he per-

suaded the Directory that he owned vast estates in Ireland and that 30,000 of the peasantry would rise the moment he set foot upon the island. He was given command of a corvette and landed on a small island off the coast of Donegal. The few fishermen who resided in the island immediately took to their boats in terror, but Tandy hoisted the Irish flag and issued a proclamation to a non-existent population urging all Irishmen "to strike from the blood-cemented thrones the murderers of their friends." Eight hours later he was carried back on board in a state of complete intoxication and the corvette sailed away to Bergen. From Bergen Tandy sought to reach Paris by land and on the evening of November 22 he reached Hamburg in a snowstorm and proceeded to the American Arms. He was there arrested by Sir James Crawford and a posse of Hamburg police and put in irons. Sir James then persuaded the Hamburg Senate to deliver over Tandy's person and embarked him upon a British man-of-war. Bonaparte, when he became First Consul, claimed that this was a violation of International Law and fined the Hamburg Senate the sum of four and a half million francs. The British Government, feeling that they were on uncertain ground, first condemned Tandy to death and then released him. He returned to France as a hero and a martyr and died of dysentery at Bordeaux.

It is not surprising that Sir James Crawford, even in 1800, should have looked upon all Irish revolutionaries with distaste. He replied to Hamilton Rowan by saying that "Lord Castlereagh's letter does not authorize you to expect those attentions usually reciprocal between British subjects and their Ministers."

Wounded by this rebuff, appalled by the high cost of living at Hamburg and conscious that it was the resort of spies and informers, he determined to leave that "emporium of merchandize and mischief" and to seek a home at Lübeck. No suitable house being there available, he returned to the Hamburg district and finally established himself and his family at

Altona, in "a pretty house at the end of the town" in the Grosse
Berg Strasse. During the three years of their residence at
Altona two further children were born.

He refused resolutely to associate himself with the Irish
refugees or the French agents who infested Hamburg, telling
them that he was "sick of politics." This prudent attitude was
duly reported to London by "Lord Downshire's friend." In
June of 1802, however, some of his former friends, including
Samuel Neilson who had been implicated in the 1798 rebellion
and interned for four years at Fort St. George, arrived upon
their release at Cuxhaven. Hamilton Rowan wrote to Neilson
offering "such services as he was capable of rendering." Neilson replied in a letter which does him credit. "You," he wrote,
"are, I know, delicately situated; but the purity of your views
and the integrity of your heart lead me to speak with confidence; at the same time as I wish of all things to avoid the
most remote possibility of implicating you." Hamilton Rowan
was no further implicated. And when peace was declared between England and France in 1802 his hopes of obtaining a
free pardon revived.

Meanwhile his financial affairs became inextricably involved.
He was unable, being still under sentence of outlawry, to touch
his main income, and was reduced to living upon such meagre
rents as his less intractable tenants were willing to pay. On
leaving Ireland for Germany Mrs. Hamilton Rowan had appointed as their agent a Mr. Archibald Hamilton who, although no relation, had for long been a trusted dependent of
the family. This agent indulged in billbroking on his own
account with the result that in 1809 he was declared a bankrupt. His assignees brought an action against Hamilton Rowan
alleging that he had caused their client's ruin by drawing bills
while in exile. Hamilton Rowan had from the first offered
to compound for the sum of £1,500 and the court in the end
decided that this offer was equitable and sufficient. It is, however, from the evidence tendered on both sides in the case, an
abstract of which has been preserved in the Helen's Tower Li-

brary, that I have obtained a side-light upon the distressing financial and domestic circumstances which embittered his sojourn in Altona.

Almost from the day of her arrival in Germany Mrs. Hamilton Rowan wrote peremptory letters to her agent informing him that they were "starving in a foreign land." Hamilton Rowan evidently found some difficulty in imposing economy upon his family. "I have stated," he writes, "to Mrs. Hamilton Rowan that we must reduce our expenses to some £600 per annum. This she treats as an impossibility without some exertion but what line to take neither she nor I can devise, so that our conversations on this head seldom end without a warmth that should never take place between two persons so sincerely united in friendship and interest as we are. I have tried calico printing; let her try something else." "In three weeks," he writes again, "we have twice changed cooks and have now taken a Frenchman. The fact is I have always lived in too high a style and my family do not like to give up indulgence. But what is to become of the children? Have we the wherewithal to put them in any decent line of profession? No. And we are too fond of our rank in life to make them tradesmen. My God! I would rather dig and delve if anyone would hire my body than be thus eternally on thorns."

In his desperation he thought out many devices. He thought of returning to America and buying an estate in Louisiana, but was deterred by the thought of killing Indians and owning slaves. "Some how or other," he writes, "I think a judgment falls on every place in which slavery is encouraged." He thought even of returning to Ireland and surrendering himself for trial. But here again, there was the danger that he might be sent to Botany Bay. "As to the evidence against me," he writes, "if there were much less than there must be, I would not trust to that; and what I really fear is that they would neither hang nor pardon me, but as a mark of leniency make me travel at the expense of the nation."

The Peace of Amiens revived his hopes. Had not Lord Clare himself assured Mrs. Hamilton Rowan that all would be much easier once the war was over? Lord Clare, it was true, had since died; but Lord Castlereagh, "handsome Robert Stewart," was still friendly, influential and alive. Through the good offices of his old Westminster friend Thomas Steele, then Paymaster General, he submitted a petition for clemency, couched in dignified and outright terms. He was informed by Lord Castlereagh that he was free to come to England on condition that he entered into an undertaking not to set foot in Ireland. An English pardon, Lord Castlereagh assured him, might now without great difficulty be obtained; a pardon under the great seal of Ireland was more problematical since "it would give great offence especially to the aristocracy." Relying on these promises he crossed to England and arrived in London on June 16, 1803. He rented No. 58 Sloane Street, where he remained with his family for a period of two years.

## (2)

One of his more galling preoccupations during this period was the condition into which his father had relapsed. Old Baldie was then some seventy-five years of age and had fallen completely under the domination of his mistress, Ursula Carlisle, by whom he had had an illegitimate son. Hamilton Rowan was much worried lest the old man might be bullied into transferring to Ursula and her son such of the property at Killyleagh and Killinchey as was not entailed. These anxieties were not diminished by the reports he received from his agent, Archibald Hamilton. "Ursula," reported the latter, "is a woman of uncommon violence of temper and that violence is considerably inflamed by intoxication; when in that state she is outrageous even to desperation. The servants in the house partake of her good cheer, the humbler neighbours also partake, and the consequence is that she is supported in all her designs by those around her."

Old Baldie, in the early months of 1805, had decided to cross to London and to visit his son and grandchildren in Sloane Street. Hamilton Rowan looked forward to this visit with some apprehension. "Why," he wrote to his agent, "did I wish for his arrival? I know not; for the unfortunate situation which we live in, I mean with regard to domestic ease, is ill suited to anyone, and will perhaps be more irksome to him, from that very placidity which marks his character."

When the old man arrived, however, it was clear that he was very ill indeed. Hamilton Rowan feared that if he died while Ursula was in possession of the castle she might seize the plate, the jewels and the title deeds for herself and her son. He warned his agent who paid a surprise visit to Killyleagh and collected all the papers and valuables into the muniment room at the foot of one of the towers, which he locked and sealed. Old Baldie died on April 9 and Hamilton Rowan sent an express to his agent instructing him to take possession of the castle immediately. This precaution was justified. The agent happened fortunately to be in Belfast when the express arrived. He galloped off to Killyleagh arriving there before the news had reached the town. He secured the help of the local volunteers whom he picketed outside the muniment room and in the passage leading to the closet where the silver was stored. He then went upstairs to break the news to Ursula. "The unfortunate woman," he recorded later, "on hearing of her master's death became absolutely deranged. She shrieked so as to be heard at a remote part of the town; she tore her hair; beat her head against the wall; and tumbled herself completely down the grand staircase of the castle screaming abuse in a most horrid manner." They managed to push her out of the hall door and to close and bolt the door behind her; she remained sitting on the steps, yelling out that rather than that Hamilton Rowan, "that infamous son of a bitch," should inherit the castle she would herself set fire to the powder magazine "and blow herself and the castle to hell." She was removed by force to her sister's house in the town and her per-

sonal effects were sent after her. Her son, who was absent at
the time, behaved with greater discretion. He asked only to
be sent a small chest that was in the dining room, "and the old
dog Dob and a son of his, Bumper."

It now became all the more important for Hamilton Rowan
to obtain a reversal of his outlawry and the right to enjoy his
fortune and his estates. Lord Castlereagh exerted all his influence and an agreement was reached with the Irish authorities
upon a form of procedure which, although humiliating, was
not intolerable. Hamilton Rowan crossed to Dublin on June
13, 1805. His agent drove down to the Pigeon House to meet
him and Hamilton Rowan waved in greeting as the packet slid
along the quay. They drove together to the agent's house in
Dominick Street, the very street from which, on a May midnight eleven years ago, Hamilton Rowan had escaped. A few
days later he attended at the Court of King's Bench. The
Clerk of the Crown asked him to show cause why judgment of
death and execution should not be awarded against him. He
pleaded His Majesty's pardon, being obliged to do so kneeling upon his knees. He was allowed to make a short statement.
He spoke as follows:

"When I last had the honour of appearing before this tribunal
I told your Lordships that I knew His Majesty only by his wield-
ing the force of the country; since that period, during my legal
incapacity and absence beyond seas, my wife and children have
not only been unmolested, but protected; and in addition to
these favours I am now indebted to the Royal Mercy for my life.
I will neither, My Lords, insist upon the rectitude of my intentions, nor the extent of my gratitude, since these might be attributed to base and unworthy motives; but I hope my future life
will evince the sincerity of those feelings with which I am
impressed by such unmerited proofs of His Majesty's benefi-
cence."

Chief Justice Downes then pronounced that the sentence of
outlawry had been reversed, at which Hamilton Rowan bowed
three times to the Court and withdrew.

He may well have supposed that after this galling ceremony all his troubles were ended. He had, however, forgotten Dowell, the jailer whom, on that night of May 1, 1794, he had tricked into accompanying him to Dominick Street. Dowell had discovered that, although the sentence of outlawry had been removed, the former sentence of two years' imprisonment for uttering seditious libel remained in force and that technically Hamilton Rowan was still his prisoner. Accompanied by the Sheriff and intent upon his revenge he demanded that Hamilton Rowan should at once be lodged in Newgate. Fortunately his friends had foreseen some such episode, had hurried him quickly out of court, and had lodged him in the room of the Chief Secretary, Mr. Marsden, in Dublin Castle. For a moment Hamilton Rowan was appalled by this reverse of fortune. "No—by God!" he shouted, "I have been tricked; this is a scheme." Mr. Marsden intervened. He persuaded the Sheriff to agree that "he would not take cognizance of the fact that Mr. Hamilton Rowan was still technically in his custody." He persuaded Dowell to withdraw and the vindictiveness of the latter was subsequently assuaged by the gift of a large sum of money.

Hamilton Rowan, on July 21, 1805, returned as a free man to London. Although his financial affairs were still in some disorder he felt that he could afford to be extravagant. He gave William Godwin, the esurient widower of his old friend Mary Wollstonecraft, a present of £450. He bought a magnificent carriage, "with leather squabs and rumble tumbles" for the sum of £220. He engaged a chef-butler, a footman and a lady's maid. He bought four elegant bay horses. He paid Mr. Sweetman £100 for the boat he had borrowed. The claims of the Sheridan brothers and of Murphy were at length adjusted. He made generous provisions for Ursula and her son. And he prepared to return to Ireland in triumph.

(3)

On July 27, 1806, he crossed with his wife, his children, his servants, his carriages and his horses to Donaghadee. His neighbour and cousin, Lord Dufferin, had strongly advised him against "anything in the nature of a demonstration." Hamilton Rowan none the less was determined to return to his home in triumph. All preparations had been left in the hands of his agent, Archibald Hamilton, who in the subsequent action which was brought against his patron gave a highly coloured version of what occurred. His record is more detailed than that published in the Irish newspapers, and I therefore quote it as it stands:

"Nothing could exceed the pomp and ceremony. Crowds of persons, in spite of all restraint, advanced two miles from the town of Killyleagh whilst multitudes remained about a mile from it. The signal of his approach at length being given the air resounded with shouts of joy. At length the cavalcade appeared in view, when the shouts were again renewed and continued without interruption. Hundreds of horsemen preceded the procession; Mr. Hamilton Rowan's servants came first in his post chaise; then the hero of the scene, mounted in an exceedingly high phaeton; then his barouche with his wife and children drawn by four elegant bays; then horsemen and pedestrians.

"On his joining the populace who had posted themselves nearest the town, he descended and saluted them. Ropes were then fastened to the carriage and all the family were drawn triumphantly into the town—except Mrs. Hamilton Rowan who very sensibly observed that she would not be drawn by human creatures who could debase themselves to the rank of beasts; and whom she was convinced would far more cheerfully draw Ursula in triumph than herself.

"When Mr. Hamilton Rowan entered the town, the bells of the church, which had lately tolled his father's funeral, now rang for joy at the son's arrival. All the inhabitants greeted him and, arrived at the castle, he again saluted the multitude, and entered to partake of the repast which had been prepared for him and his family.

"Hamilton Rowan on approaching the castle was very much affected indeed. The scene was impressive to an extreme. After so long an absence—an absence which but a short time before he thought was to be for ever—after so many years of exile and misfortune—once more to enter the seat of his ancestors and to enter it as its proprietor and lord-absolved-restored-renewed-triumphant—'twas not to be easily borne. He melted into tears. He gazed in silence at every object as he passed. Not one word—until on reaching the great parlour the family paintings struck his eye. He turned to his agent, Archibald Hamilton, amidst the surrounding crowd of visitors, and grasping him by both hands, and looking for a while alternatively at the paintings and his deliverer, exclaimed, 'It is to you, my good friend, that I owe all this.'

"The evening was spent in mirth and gaiety. The town was brilliantly illuminated. Even the ships in the harbour had lantherns affixed to the tops of their masts. Fireworks were displayed in great variety the whole of the night; bonfires covered the surrounding hills; and the numerous country people who attended were amply regaled with beer, porter and meat."

Thus did Hamilton Rowan return at last to Killyleagh.

(4)

Lord Dufferin may have been correct in deprecating any ostentatious demonstration. Unlike so many of his actions, Hamilton Rowan's triumphal home-coming had, however, been staged with deliberate forethought. "We shall come over," he had written to his agent, "completely and rather elegantly caparisoned, since the first impression always goes a great way." It was necessary perhaps that such an impression should be created. It was necessary to expunge from the memory of the citizens of Killyleagh the picture of Ursula yelling drunken blasphemies upon the castle steps. It was necessary to expunge from his own mind the memories of Newgate, of Mr. Sweetman's pleasure boat, of the galley slaves in Brest prison, of the thud of the guillotine, of the beer-barrels at Wilmington. It was necessary for him to forget that he had knelt in the dock at the Court of King's Bench and humbly sued for pardon. It was necessary to remember that he was now a man of great possessions.

His former confederates had been less fortunate. Thirty-four of the original members of the Society of United Irishmen had died on the gallows, and countless others whom their example or guidance had tempted into rebellion had been executed or killed. Tone had cut his throat with a pen-knife while awaiting execution; Edward Fitzgerald had died miserably of wounds received while resisting arrest; Russell had been hanged at Downpatrick for complicity in the rising of Robert Emmet; Napper Tandy, after covering himself with public ridicule, had died at Bordeaux; Oliver Bond had died in Kilmainham jail; Reynolds, having been exposed as an informer, had died of cholera at Lisbon "hid beneath the heap of his own carnage"; Simon Butler had died in Brompton Row; Samuel Neilson had died in exile at Poughkeepsie. They were all dead. Only Drennan survived, living in Belfast, writing poetry, inventing that catchy phrase "The Emerald Isle." Assuredly Hamilton Rowan was more fortunate than many.

From the towers of his castle he could look down upon the prosperous little town and out over the wide stretches of the Lough to where the sunshine struck the distant Scottish hills. His wife and daughters were around him. Three of his sons held commissions in His Majesty's forces. He could when he so desired exchange the sharp tang of Killyleagh for the softer woods and meadows of Rathcoffey. Gradually he was forgiven even by the Anglo-Irish aristocracy, "whose heads," he had once written, "will be the first to be levelled in the dust." Lord Hardwicke, it is true, had refused to receive him; but subsequent Lord Lieutenants were more willing to forget. Jonah Barrington records having "seen him and his family at the castle drawing rooms in dresses singularly splendid, where they were well received by the Viceroy and by many of the nobility and gentry." His daughters married well. His eldest son was rapidly making for himself a brilliant naval career. He was assuredly more fortunate than many.

For years he refused to associate himself with any political or social movements. "These freaks," he had written, "must end now." He bought a house in Leinster Street with a garden giving upon the premises of the Irish Royal Society. He dabbled in chemistry and installed a laboratory in his three Irish homes. He studied printing and lithography and struck off little poems translated from the French or Latin. He had great schemes for rendering Killyleagh a centre of the linen trade, he encouraged the erection of mills and built two new streets to house the work-people. The sweet smell of drying flax came to mingle with the scent of sea-weed in the Killyleagh air. The elegant, slightly foppish youth of the Wheatley portrait had been hardened by adversity into a huge and gnarled old man. He became choleric in his later years and his children regarded him with awe. But he retained his former courtesy and those who met him in his old age were startled that so soft a voice could proceed from so vast and harsh a body. "The impression he left on me," records Charles Phillipps, "was that of a warm heart, an open hand, and the kindliest nature." The "freaks" to which he was addicted were not however wholly at an end. For many years, it is true, he kept his promises to the Government and abstained from any connection with public affairs. In February 1812 he was exposed to a temptation which he nobly resisted. He received the following letter:

1 Lower Sackville Street
Dublin
*February 25, 1812.*

SIR,

Although I have not the pleasure of being personally known to you, I consider the motive which actuated me in writing the enclosed, sufficiently introductory to authorize me in sending you some copies and waving ceremonials in a case where public benefit is concerned.

Sir, although an Englishman, I feel for Ireland. I have left the country in which the chance of birth placed me, for the whole purpose of adding my little stock of usefulness to the fund which I hope Ireland possesses to aid me in the unequal but sacred combat in which she is engaged.

In the course of a few days more I shall print another small pamphlet which shall be sent to you. I have intentionally vulgarized the language of the enclosed. I have printed 1,500 copies and am now distributing them throughout Dublin.

Sir, with respect,
I am your obedient humble servant,
P. B. SHELLEY.

Dr. Hamilton Drummond, who edited the memoirs of Hamilton Rowan with an atrocious disregard of sense and veracity, asserts that "It cannot be doubted that Mr. Hamilton Rowan treated the young enthusiast with his wonted courtesy and hospitality." There is no foundation at all for this assertion. He certainly kept the letter, but he did not answer it, nor did he agree to assist in distributing either the *"Address to the Irish People"* or *"Proposals for an Association for the Regeneration of Ireland."* I cannot but feel that on this occasion my great-great-grandfather had one of his rare but fortunate escapes. Had the incident occurred but two years later; had Shelley even mentioned Godwin to him, had he confessed that he loved the daughter of Mary Wollstonecraft, I much doubt whether Hamilton Rowan's virtuous resolutions would have withstood the strain. It would have been a repetition of the intoxicating days when Tone or Edward Fitzgerald came to dinner and when the language of freedom whirled its fumes around the brain. Hamilton Rowan knew Godwin, but having given that greedy old man a large sum of money when he could ill afford it, I doubt whether his esteem for the philosopher was wholly unmixed. It is strange only that he should have preserved Shelley's letter among the papers in the damp dark tower room at Killyleagh.

Gradually, although not disastrously, his earlier resolution began to become frayed. As one might well have expected he was a strong supporter of Queen Caroline and could not resist signing a petition on her behalf to the Lord Lieutenant. He became interested in Unitarianism and insisted upon expounding his new theory from the pulpit of Killyleagh Church. He was much incensed to observe the congregation creep out one by one until he was left alone, enormous and angry, surveying empty pews. He espoused the cause of the Dublin lamplighters; he wrote an angry letter to the newspapers about the wrongs of the silk-weavers. He became a subscribing member of the Catholic Association. In sending this subscription he wrote, and published, an indiscreet letter to Lord Fingal. "One law," he wrote, "ought to bind Catholic and Protestant, Jew and Mohammedan, if Irishmen. This has ever been my creed and will ever be my rule of action." It was this letter, which some years later, involved him in the final fantastic episode of his career.

(5)

On February 14, 1825, a debate took place at Westminster on the subject of the Catholic Association. Mr. Dawson alluded to the fact that when the names of the subscribers had been read out at a public meeting in Dublin the name of Hamilton Rowan had been received with acclamation. "The name," said Mr. Dawson, "of this convicted traitor was received with thunders of applause—and why? In order that the recollection of the disastrous period with which that name was connected might be revived in the minds of the deluded peasantry and help the designs of this abominable association."

Sir Robert Peel, in the same debate, censured the Catholic Association for having passed a vote of thanks to Hamilton Rowan whom he referred to as "an attainted traitor." Hely Hutchinson and Brougham rose in his defence. "There is not a man," said the latter, "more dearly beloved in Ireland. If to hold Mr. Hamilton Rowan an object of affection and respect be a crime, then we are all guilty."

On reading this debate, which obtained much publicity in the Irish papers, Hamilton Rowan decided that Brougham's defence was inadequate and that his own honour and that of his family had been tarnished. Although he was then seventy-four years of age he insisted upon crossing to London and demanding a personal explanation of Mr. Dawson. He was encouraged in this enterprise by Sir George Cockburn of Shanganagh Castle whose only child had married Hamilton Rowan's eldest son. The latter, hearing of the episode while serving with the fleet in the Levant, also applied for leave in order to assist his father in the battle. His leave was not granted.

Sir George Cockburn, fearing that Hamilton Rowan might find it difficult when in London to obtain seconds for his duel, offered to accompany the old man. Hamilton Rowan refused such assistance. He crossed the Irish Channel, accompanied only by his groom and personal manservant, Patrick Daly. "I will challenge him myself," he assured Sir George Cockburn, "and take out Daly as my second: he will see fair play."

On reaching London he wrote to Mr. Dawson in terms which were, as Dr. Hamilton Drummond records, "of more strength than suavity." Mr. Dawson had no desire whatsoever to fight a duel with an old man of seventy-four. He appealed to his friend Lord Hotham to arrange the difficulty. Lord Hotham was evidently a person of manners and resource. Hamilton Rowan described him as "a polite young man in the

Guards, cool, clear and temperate who acted in a most gentle-manlike manner." Lord Hotham managed to induce Hamilton Rowan to withdraw the insulting letter which he addressed to Mr. Dawson. He then induced Mr. Dawson to write to Hamilton Rowan assuring him the expressions he had used were "due to a consideration of public duty" and that he had had no intention "to wound your feelings or to offer you any premeditated insult." Hamilton Rowan was content with this explanation and returned in triumph to Ireland. "Thus terminated," he records, "a disagreeable affair, forced upon me by the manners of the world."

He wrote a full description of the episode to his friend William Poole, whom he had nursed through the yellow fever at Wilmington. The old quaker did not approve of "thy (foolish shall I call it?) expedition to England." "To old men such as we are," he added, "it appears to me to be of much more importance to preserve the quietude and innocence of our minds than to take a very deep interest of any kind in a world from which we are soon to pass away."

Hamilton Rowan was certainly an old man, but he had no intention for the moment of passing away. He lived on for nine happy years. His last appearance in public was on January 20, 1829, when he attended a meeting in the Rotunda organized by the Friends of Civil and Religious Liberty.

On leaving the building he was recognized by the crowd in Sackville Street, who drew him in a final mob triumph to his home.

His wife died in February 1834 and in the following August his eldest son was stricken with sudden death. He was unable to survive these disasters. He died quietly on November 1, 1834, in the eighty-fourth year of his age.

# EPILOGUE

## (1)

IN THE year 1920 my eldest brother was stationed with his regiment, the XVth Hussars, in Marlborough Barracks, Dublin. A party of English recruits had been sent into the town one morning to draw their bread ration at a bakery. They were young recruits—mere boys from Kent or Sussex who had not known the First German War. As the bread was being loaded into the lorry a group of young men who were sauntering by suddenly whipped out revolvers and opened fire upon the English soldiers. Three of their number were either killed or mortally wounded. The sergeant in charge of the party was also armed with a revolver and with the assistance of a lance-corporal captured one of the assailants who had hidden behind a cart. His name was Kevin Barry, a lad of eighteen years. He was driven back to Marlborough Barracks and lodged in the guard-house. His trial was held in the library of the barracks and he was sentenced to death. The following night he was removed under strong guard to Mountjoy Prison where a gallows had been erected. The hangman arrived from England.

On the day of the execution Dublin went into mourning. The shops were closed, the newspapers appeared with wide black borders and an enormous crowd gathered outside the prison waiting for the hour to strike. My brother's regiment had been confined to barracks, but a few of the officers were allowed into the town on condition that they wore civilian clothes. My brother (to whom the Irish troubles were a source of unhappiness and doubt greater than anything he had endured during four long years of war) went to Mountjoy Prison and mingled with the crowd. He had seen Kevin

Barry during his trial—a white-faced lad walking bravely from
the guard-room to the library. He had seen his parents when
they visited him to say good-bye. The crowd around the
prison gates numbered many tens of thousands; there were
priests among them and children and women kneeling on the
ground, telling their beads and mumbling anguished prayers.
There was a man with a tray passing in and out among the
kneeling people selling rosaries and other mementoes of the
occasion. He had a pile of cotton handkerchiefs bearing the
semblance of young Kevin Barry surrounded by the portraits
of former Irish heroes. There was Tone, and there Edward
Fitzgerald, and there Emmet, and there Napper Tandy.
There also was Hamilton Rowan. My brother bought the
handkerchief and hid it in a drawer.

It seems strange to me that more than a century after his
death Hamilton Rowan should still be classed among the
heroes. I quite see that the Irish memory is different in quality
from the English memory. The Irish, owing to their sensi-
tiveness to legend, have small sense of history. The English,
owing to their ready acceptance of their history (which is little
more than a record of all favourable fact) have small sense
of legend. But even admitting this, I cannot really understand why an intelligent and independent nation should ven-
erate the United Irishmen so deeply and so long. Tone, certainly, was a remarkable man, but he was not in any technical
sense a United Irishman. The charm and glamour of Edward
Fitzgerald were immense, but he was never a member of the
Society. There were doubtless among them men of courage,
unselfishness and even wisdom. But many were treacherous,
many were cowardly and many backed out of the movement
the moment it became dangerous. Nor to a practical mind,
is it apparent what actual benefits the United Irishmen con-
ferred upon their country. They certainly helped to destroy
the legend of Grattan's Constitution and of Grattan's Parliament; that may have been a useful thing to have done or it
may have been a harmful thing. They were certainly instru-
mental in giving to the helpless peasantry a sense of urgency

which they had not possessed before, and a hope of liberation which at the time was unlikely to be realized. To that extent they were responsible for the unnecessary and blood-stained rising of 1798. To that extent also they were responsible for the Act of Union.

Much as I like the Irish, deeply though I wish them well, I regret that the proportions between their memory and their forgetfulness, between their forgiveness and their rancour, should be so disarranged.

Yet when I force myself to see the story through Irish eyes I do in fact catch some twilight glimmer of what they mean. The effect of any movement of liberation is not to be judged by its immediate success; the United Irishmen, whatever may have been their errors of judgment or of conduct, were in fact the first to bring to Ireland some taper-lights from the vast beacons which had been kindled in America and France; they were the first to proclaim that Grattan's Constitution and Grattan's Parliament were an imposition and a sham; they were the first, after all, to preach the ideal of a United Ireland. I see also that Hamilton Rowan has some claim to a small niche in their Valhalla. It is true that he withdrew from the contest; it is true that in the end he was conquered by his duty to his family and his great possessions; it is true that he knelt in the dock and craved for pardon. But even he, in his mild wild way, brought some truth into darkness; even he gave what at the time was an astonishing example to his fellows among the Protestant Ascendancy; and even he endured long and bitter suffering for the rights of a religion and a race which were not his own.

I am glad that his portrait, printed in green ink upon a calico handkerchief, should figure among the heroes.

(2)

The mutual antipathy which exists between the logical and the illogical mind is apt to blur understanding. I am perhaps unduly irritated by the fact that my great-great-grandfather attributed more importance to his premises than he did to their conclusions, and that his career was, to say the least, hampered by an undistributed middle. Yet logical consistency is the least attractive of all consistencies, and his consistency of spirit was undeviating and superb. I should feel happier about him were I convinced that he loved Ireland as much as he loved his own opinions or even that he hated oppression as much as he hated established institutions. I should feel more satisfied if I believed that his rebelliousness was inspired by some clear vision of what he wanted to construct, rather than by a hazy notion of what he wished to destroy. I should be more content with him were it not for a suspicion that his moral courage was less sturdy than his physical courage and that he plunged into extreme courses for fear lest, if he paused to ponder, he might wish to retreat. I should understand him better had he taken serious people more seriously or fallen a less easy victim to the unreliable. I should have respected him more had not the fact that his life was dominated by two managing women rendered him so unmanageable. And I should be proud of him indeed, were I certain in my own mind that the sufferings which he bore with such good humour had been borne without a touch of self-dramatization or had been incurred from motives more constant and more serious than that of a desire to please.

To his descendants he has handed down many of his virtues and many of his faults. He has bequeathed a shattered mirror, in each fragment of which I can see reflected some facet of his weakness or his strength. To some of them he bequeathed his patrician manners and appearance; to others his essential gentleness of spirit; to some his generous warmth of sympathy; to others his contradictory, or even his combative frame of mind; to some his gift of pity; to others again his inability to deal objectively with external events. To almost all of them he transmitted a marked incompetence in mundane affairs, a lack of skill or care in the management of private finance, a sad legacy of impatience and impulsiveness, a deficiency of caution, an intermittent interest in the struggle for success; a dreadful tendency to think by fits and starts.

Particularly illustrative for me of this distributed heritage was my uncle Gawen Rowan Hamilton of Killyleagh. He was the handsomest man of his age that I have ever seen. He was tall and thin and brown; he had a nose like the beak of a hawk and the presence of a Rajput King. His clothing tended towards that of 1830, as did his accent and his voice. His hats, which were faintly Regency in shape, were always the same colour as his clothes. He wore when in the country a beautifully arranged ivory stock secured with a pink coral pin. He was a restless man and one who would spend his days doing nothing with aloof deliberation. He would walk into a room, stare angrily at its occupant, and then walk out again without a word. His wife was impersonal, at least to governesses and children, in a different manner. She was artistic, musical, interested in theosophy, a subscriber to the Yellow Book, a collector of Aubrey Beardsley drawings. Her eyelashes would flutter absently as the wings of a butterfly which has settled on a flower which it does not really like. My uncle would drag the poor woman from Killyleagh to London, from London to Brighton in a constant stately escape from his own boredom. He never even remotely understood the difference between capital and income. As a child I was alarmed by my uncle and my aunt. In later years I came to understand and like them both. My uncle would translate Kipling's "Recessional" into Latin elegiacs and send them to me to correct before passing them on to the *Belfast News Letter* or *The Times*. I was flattered by this attention; and it was my aunt who, to the displeasure of my immediate family, gave me a transient taste for the works of Oscar Wilde.

My uncle was not interested in politics. As a young man he had been in the Dragoons, and indeed he looked the part. He was gifted in his way but devoid of application. He played small part in Irish controversies, referred but seldom to the Land League, and appeared bored by all current issues. But when the home-rule controversy blazed up in 1913 he suddenly aroused himself from his torpor. Once again, in the wide courtyard of Killyleagh, the Volunteers were drilled.

But not for the purposes of a United Ireland.

Only once, since the Treaty, have I been to Killyleagh. I wandered alone through the deserted garden in search of the past, seeking to explain to myself the underlying antipathy that I felt. Was it that my reason rebelled against the dissensions which those towers had witnessed and which I could neither understand nor share? Or was it that my nerves vibrated again to my old night terrors, when the wind from the sea would hoot round the battlements, and I lay there thinking of so many grandfathers and great-grandfathers buried in the marine cemetery above the Lough?

Yet even in those nervous childhood days there had been summer mornings when I was wakened by the siren of the linen factory in the little town; when from my turret window I saw the indented shadow of the battlements slanting across the fore-court; when the scent of sea-weed mingled with the sickly breath of flax drying in the fields; and when I looked down over tumbled roofs climbing up to the castle gate-house, and traced the early smoke of chimneys down the steep street, to where, from the small harbour, the creak of spars, the voices of fishermen, reached me in the soundless air. Beyond them, beyond the distant trees of Ardquin and Portaferry, tumbled the anxious Irish sea. June mornings when the sun first parts the haze and the white limbs of beeches stretch their muscles under windless leaves.

### (3)

In all the jumble that Hamilton Rowan made of his own life, in all the jumble that he bequeathed to his descendants, there is one clear note which rings above the discordance. His eldest son inherited all his virtues and none of his less venial faults. The gift of pity which, in Hamilton Rowan redeemed so many frailties, was in his son combined with firmness of pur-

pose and great balance of judgment.   He was able, in another
and no less glorious cause, to accomplish much that his father
had failed to achieve.   I shall end my story upon this satis-
factory note.

Commodore William Gawen Rowan Hamilton—the little
boy who was born in the Petit Hôtel de Choiseul, the little boy
who in the back bedroom at Dominick Street had seen the
gigantic figure of his father huddle through the dark window
and sink downwards on a knotted rope—had entered His Majesty's Navy at an early age.   While still a lad he had fought
in China and fought at Tobago.   He was severely wounded at
Alexandria and in the year before Trafalgar he joined the
fleet of Nelson and was personally commended by that hero
for his courage and efficiency.   As a lieutenant he was in command of a raiding party in the bay of Rosas and as a reward
for his services he became at the age of twenty-seven Captain
of the *Onyx*.   In her he served during the Peninsular War.
He patrolled outside Cadiz; he took part in the capture of
Almeida, Almunecar and Nerja; he drove the French out of
Villa Joyosa and Navis, destroyed their batteries and spiked
their guns.   In 1813 he was appointed to the *Rainbow*, sank
twenty-four enemy ships in the bay of Viareggio, was present
at the capture of Genoa and wounded at the capture of Leg-
horn.   In the American War of 1812-1814 he was present at
the attack on Baltimore and accompanied Captain Barry on his
expedition up the Rappahannock when they surprised the
enemy on land and seized their colours.   With the coming of
peace his ship was put out of commission and he was granted
indefinite leave.

He joined his parents in Ireland.   Some twenty miles from
Rathcoffey upon the sea coast in the vicinity of the little town
of Bray, was the estate of Shanganagh Castle, the property of
General Sir George Cockburn, a man of liberal opinions and
considerable fortune.   Captain Rowan Hamilton paid frequent
visits to Shanganagh and in 1817 he married the General's only
child and heiress.   It was in this manner that Shanganagh

Castle was added to the family possessions, and became in a later generation the dower house to which my grandmother retired formidably when my uncle Gawen established himself at Killyleagh.

In 1820 Captain Rowan Hamilton was appointed to the *Cambrian* and was detailed to conduct the Ambassador, Lord Strangford, to his post at Constantinople. Having fulfilled this mission, he remained in the Levant for twelve years. It was in this manner that he came to play a leading and wholly salutary part in the Greek War of Independence.

The similarity between Greek and Irish politics has often been noted. There is the same under-current of burning passion and garrulous patriotism; there is the same tendency for the leaders of the movement to quarrel among themselves, to form individual parties, and to devote to internecine struggles the energies which should be preserved for unity against the external enemy. In Greece this hereditary tendency towards fragmentation was increased by the jealousies of the Great Powers. Thus apart from the rivalries between the Greek tribal leaders and the Greek politicians, apart from the divisions between Attica, Western Greece, the Morea and the Islands, there also existed a French Party, a Russian Party and an English Party. In addition to this, individual brigands, such as Odysseus, set themselves up as local patriots upon their own. Nor was English opinion in itself unanimous. The Whigs were in favour of Greek freedom; the city merchants, and above all the English traders in the Near East, were afraid that the emergence of an independent Greece might damage the advantage they enjoyed in the Levant trade; the Cabinet in London, fearful of any disturbance of the principle of legitimacy, fearful of any increase in French or Russian influence in the Eastern Mediterranean, were inclined towards a policy of appeasement and non-intervention; and most of the British officials and officers on the spot were (as always) apt to lend too ready an ear to the solicitations of the Anglo-Levantine merchants and to persuade themselves that on the whole the Turk was the more convenient and therefore the better man.

The Philhellenes who in their hundreds flocked to assist Greece in her bitter struggle were equally divided. Some adhered to the civilian government under Mavrocordato; some joined the military chieftains in Maina or the naval privateers at Hydra and Spetzai; some discovered a small brigand bandit all on their own; and some deserted to the Turks. Never has any cause been so split by internal dissensions or fallen into such a welter of conflicting loyalties. Even the soundest head became bemused.

It can well be conceived what an appalling mess Hamilton Rowan would have made of himself had he been faced with such a situation. In seeking to please everybody he would have acquired the respect of none. Always he would have believed ardently and sincerely in the righteousness of the last primate, brigand, pirate or agent whom he happened to meet. His son was different. Among all the English Philhellenes in the Levant, among all the British officers or officials whose duty brought them into contact with the Greek War of Independence, he alone kept a cool clear head, he alone won and preserved the respect of all.

(4)

His sympathies, of course, were on the side of the Greeks; if he favoured any party, he favoured the civilian, or democratic, party of Mavrocordato, not because it was regarded as the "English Party" but because it seemed to him the only organization which could provide a central Government for Greece. He had the uttermost contempt for those Philhellenes whose sympathies for the modern Greeks were founded upon a pedantic respect for their ancestors in the Fifth Century before Christ. He and Napier, and perhaps Byron, were among the few Englishmen of the time who recognized the great qualities of the modern Greek people and who firmly believed that they were capable, if left to themselves, of establishing an independent state, orderly, civilized and progressive. He chafed, naturally, against the policy of nonintervention so timidly pursued by the Cabinet in London. "I believe," he wrote to Sir Frederick Adam, then High Commissioner in the Ionian Islands, "I believe that the English will mourn over, but not save, Greece." "I have always felt," he added, "a lively interest as to the fate of this, however savage, still Christian country; the mass of its population seems to me to be very superior to other countries; I cannot help feeling interested for such a people." His was not a merely sentimental sympathy. He interpreted his admiration and pity in concrete terms.

In the first place he sought by every means in his power to induce the several Greek factions to compose their differences. He sought also to induce the Greek rebels to behave in such a manner as would persuade Europe that they deserved the liberty they claimed. A typical instance of his influence and intervention is recorded in the first volume of Finlay's *Greek Revolution*. The Greek capitani had surrounded Nauplia and had promised that if the town surrendered, the garrison would be transported to Asia Minor and allowed to take with them one praying carpet, one quilt and one suit of clothes. The Turks capitulated and the Greeks then decided to massacre their prisoners. Finlay's account continues:

"On this occasion Greece was saved from disgrace by the arrival of an English frigate on the 24th of December. The *Cambrian* was commanded by Captain Hamilton who was already personally known to several of the Greek chiefs then present. His frank and decided conduct won the confidence of all parties. He held a conference with Colocotrones and the Moreot chieftains, whose Russian prejudices induced them to view the interference of an English officer with great jealousy. He was obliged to tell them in strong language, that if, on this occasion, they failed to take effectual measures for the honourable execution of the capitulation, they would render the Greek name despicable in civilized Europe, and perhaps ruin the cause of Greece.

"The chiefs respected Hamilton's character; the wild soldiers admired his martial bearing and the frankness with which he spoke the whole truth. He took advantage of the feeling which he had created in his favour to act with energy. He insisted on the Greek Government immediately chartering vessels to embark the Turks, and to facilitate their departure, he took five hundred on board the *Cambrian*. He thus saved the Greeks from the dishonour of violating their plighted faith, but he inflicted a great sacrifice on England. Sixty-seven of the Turks embarked on board died before reaching Smyrna. The typhus fever, which they brought on board, spread among the crew and several fell victims to the disease.

"Captain Hamilton was the first public advocate of the Greek cause among Englishmen in an influential position, and he deserves to be ranked among the greatest benefactors of Greece."

It was not only his espousal of their cause or his insistence upon their good conduct which has given to Captain Hamilton and the *Cambrian* so high a repute in the annals of modern Greece. During these twelve years he devoted himself unsparingly to the rescue of Greek refugees from Turkish massacre and he spent a large part of his personal fortune in ransoming Greek captives. To his efforts alone was due the rescue of many thousands of Greek women and children. I am glad to know that he was present at the Battle of Navarino and thus witnessed the act of liberation for which, during all those years, he had scarcely dared to hope. And when I visit Athens it is with pride that I walk down the street which bears his name.

When the independence of Greece had been recognized by the Great Powers, Commodore Hamilton returned to Ireland. He was received at Killyleagh with rejoicing and once again the little town was illuminated and the lights of rockets and Bengal fire glittered in the Lough. On passing under the castle gateway his horse took fright and he was thrown from his carriage. He received internal injuries and died a few weeks later in the presence of his father, his wife and his two schoolboy sons.

(5)

Sir George Cockburn of Shanganagh Castle, father-in-law to Commodore Rowan Hamilton, was not merely a retired general; he was an ardent Whig politician; he was also a collector of antiquities. When stationed in Sicily after the defeat of General Cavaignac's division he had amused himself by collecting a number of Greek and Roman relics, including a large porphyry bath and many funeral urns, which on his return to Shanganagh he arranged in a special room called the "Monumental Room." This room stood between the ballroom and the dining room, deriving from its neighbours the smell, on the one hand of damp walls and ivy, and on the other hand of peaches and marsala.

Captain Rowan Hamilton, while cruising during all those years among the islands of the Aegean, would from time to time recall the tastes of his father-in-law and send back to Shanganagh, now the fragment of an Ionic column, now some shattered inscription from Nauplia or Epidaurus. On one occasion he had found (it may well have been among the deserted stones of Delos) four Greek altars of marble on which were carved rich swags of grape, of pomegranate, and myrtle suspended between the heads of bulls. I can picture the sailors of the *Cambrian* in their tarpaulin hats rolling these great drums of marble down to the beach at Delos and hoisting them with ropes and tackle upon the frigate's deck. Eventually these altars arrived at Shanganagh in the company of a Corinthian capital of later date. They were too large to house in the Monumental Room and Sir George Cockburn decided to erect them one on top of the other as a column commemorative of the Reform Bill.

A site was chosen in front of the main entrance. A wide base was built from Irish granite in the shape of four high ascending steps. Upon this base a granite drum was inserted and on the top of it the four altars rose successively in the air surmounted by the Corinthian capital. Into the face of the top step Sir George inserted a marble tablet bearing the following inscription:

This Column erected
in July 1832
by
General Sir George Cockburn, G.C.H.
to commemorate
THE REFORM BILLS
passed this year
is formed of ancient Greek marbles
(the granite base excepted)
sent him from the
Levant
by his son-in-law
Captain W. G. Hamilton, R.N.

Around the foot of the column there was a wide square of gravel, separated from the surrounding turf by high granite piers joined to each other by hanging chains. It was a delight to me as a child to swing upon those chains, chanting little songs, watching the white clouds sail above the Wicklow mountains and the cows munching at the buttercups around. Up and down I used to swing, my hanging feet making little paw marks in the careful gravel below; my song echoing in the summer air.

When my grandmother died in 1919 my uncle Gawen, in a moment of impatience, suddenly sold Shanganagh with all its contents. In 1936 it again came into the market, and being anxious to rescue some at least of the memories of my childhood, I crossed to Dublin and attended the sale. I bought the column as it stood and had the altars and the top tier of the base transported to my home at Sissinghurst. Three of the altars and the Corinthian capital were disposed, with some ungainliness, along a garden path. The fourth, with the base and the inscription, was erected in the orchard.

As a liberal and a democrat I share Sir George Cockburn's appreciation of the Reform Bills of 1832. I rejoice that they and Greece should jointly if incongruously be commemorated between the wild roses and the apple tree. I gaze at the white marble tablet with satisfaction. But on the back of the monument, in darker stone, Sir George Cockburn has inserted another and less contented inscription. It runs as follows:

July 1838
Alas
To this day
a Hum Bug.

# ABRIDGED GENEALOGY

James Hamilton of Killyleagh
created Viscount Clandeboye
1559–1643

James Hamilton
created Earl of Clanbrassil
d. 1639

Henry Hamilton
2nd Earl of Clanbrassil
Poisoned by his wife Alice Moore 1675
[no issue survived]

ARCHIBALD HAMILTON ROWAN
1751–1834
married Sarah Dawson
had ten children

Commodore Gawen William Rowan Hamilton
1793–1834
married Catherine d. of Sir George Cockburne
of Shanganagh Castle

Archibald Rowan Hamilton
1817–1860
married Catherine d. of Rev. Charles Caldwell
who died in her 99th year (1919) leaving issue :—

Hariot
married Marquis of Dufferin and Ava

Gawen  George

Archibald Hamilton
of Halcraig

[Four other sons]

Gawen Hamilton
of Killyleagh
1630–1703

Archibald Hamilton
of Killyleagh
d. 1747

Gawen Hamilton
of Killyleagh
1729–1805
married Jane Rowan
dow of Tichborne Aston
nly child of William Rowan

Sidney
married Rev. Benjamin Beresford
[two children]

ndoline     Frederick          Mary Catherine
married Arthur Nicolson
First Lord Carnock

# INDEX